Humor and Eloquence in Public Speaking

Humor and Eloquence in Public Speaking

Edward J. Hegarty

PARKER PUBLISHING COMPANY, INC.
West Nyack, N.Y.

Also by the Author

Making What You Say Pay Off
How to Talk Your Way to the Top

Parker Publishing Company, Inc.

West Nyack, N.Y.

Library of Congress Cataloging in Publication Data

Hegarty, Edward J
Humor and eloquence in public speaking.

1. Public speaking. 2. Wit and humor--History and criticism. 3. Eloquence. I. Title.
PN4066.H4 808.5'1 76-20439
ISBN 0-13-447896-7

Printed in the United States of America

WHAT THIS BOOK WILL DO FOR YOU

During a lifetime of more than fifty years as a public speaker, teacher of public speaking courses, and an observer of countless thousands of public speeches, I have concluded that it is the presence of two key elements, humor and eloquence, that helps to insure the success of any speech. The addition of humor and eloquence to a speech calls for certain skills, and this book helps you to develop and perfect these skills.

Over the years in my speaking courses, students have told me, "I could never be humorous," while others argued, "I'd feel ridiculous trying to be eloquent." Following the advice and techniques offered in this book, both types of students have proven to themselves that they could indeed be humorous and eloquent in their public speaking. If you have shared the students' doubts about your ability to inject humor and eloquence into your speeches, think of the pleasure you'll have in discovering–

How quickly you solve the problem of starting. Turn to Chapter 25 and select from the 12 suggested plans. You can handle any one of them easily.

Note: Turn to Chapter 25 now and see the variety of starts available to you. Each chapter offers similar helps.

Now for humor–ten kinds of humor listed in Chapter 4. There is also advice on the kinds you can use in good taste.

How to have fun finding humor material. Do your own research, easily and fast. Get the methods from Chapter 5.

Chapter 6 and 7 show how to translate a story from printed language to speaking words. You'll find ten details to check.

Want to know six ways to put your feelings into an eloquent appeal for your cause, project, or candidate? You'll find tested plans in Chapter 9.

It's easy to make listeners a part of your speech; Chapter 10 helps by showing how to use their wants and desires to strengthen your appeals to them.

Words are your tools. Learn the easy way to select the best words for strengthening your appeal. You'll find out how to use these words in phrases, questions and sentences to help shape the thinking of listeners. It's all in Chapter 11.

According to Chapter 12 the world is full of sources of eloquence you can use. Note the suggestions for making notes and filing material you'd feel comfortable using.

The ideas for building eloquent speech units are found in Chapter 13. Cover these four simple steps and you'll have units that make your speech more effective.

Too much is too much says Chapter 14. This applies to both humor and eloquence. The advice helps you judge how much to use.

If you have ever tried to tell a funny story and had disappointing results, Chapter 15 will tell you why and explain how to avoid such trouble in the future.

How can you get humor or eloquence out of figures or visuals? Chapter 20 and 21 describe many ways.

Most good speakers you hear use some dramatics in producing humor or eloquence. How they do it is explained in Chapter 22.

You've seen speakers get the audience into speeches by action, by speaking, or helping. Devices to do this are given in Chapter 23.

Ways to end your speech with humor or eloquence? Chapter 25 gives you sixteen ideas. Select any one that fits your personality and don't be surprised if you get a standing ovation.

There are hundreds of ideas in these chapters for polishing your speeches. Read through any of the chapters and convince yourself that you too can use any of the ideas suggested.

The methods of selecting, developing and using material work because they are ones used by professional speakers, women and men who charge high fees for their speeches. You won't find much theory in them. It is all "how-to." Try any one of them and see how well it works for you. Hundreds of my speech students tell me how successful they have become. One put it, "I am now the kind of speaker listeners like." Another said, "I use humor and eloquence without hesitation." A young lady said, "You used to tell me I acted scared when I spoke, but not any more. I use humor and eloquence and the boss is giving me a spot at his weekly meetings."

GO FOR THE BIG COMPLIMENT

When listeners compliment you on a speech, you want more than, "Good speech." You want such praise as, "Humor comes easy to you, doesn't it?" or, "You're so enthusiastic some of your zeal rubs off on me." You can go for such bouquets. It means some work, but think of the rewards–

Listeners have more respect for you.

They feel you are more competent.

You advance faster in your business or profession.

You become a leader in civic activities.

You move up in club and fraternal work.

You see skilled speakers getting the better jobs, the hurrahs, the honors. Why not join them? Why be an average speaker when you can be one of the best?

An improvement plan is laid out for you in the chapters ahead. Good luck!

Ed J. Hegarty

CONTENTS

Part One

HOW TO FIND AND HANDLE HUMOR

Smiles, laughs, hilarity.

All indicate approval for the speaker.

They show he can unbend, be human, be one of the group.

And so most speakers try for humor. Some find the laughs come easily. Others find them more difficult. Any speaker can develop the ability to fit humor into his material. I say this from experience in training speakers. So many have told me, "There's no sense in my trying to be humorous. I just haven't got it."

After working with them on devices to produce laughs, they developed an easy facility in this area. The laughs you hear in most speeches are brought on by these popular vehicles:

1. Accounts of the speaker's personal experience
2. The gag, wise crack, or one-liner, and
3. The humorous story.

KEEP IT SIMPLE

The job of being humorous is easier because everyday happenings bring most laughs. I once heard the late George S. Kaufman say, "The funny things in life are simple–pickles, salami, Brooklyn." Sam Levenson added, "And snoring." Check the speakers that make listeners laugh and you'll find they understand that simple things are humorous to all.

The ideas in the chapters in this part of the book show how speakers find humor, how they get it ready for use, and how they handle it.

I

THE EASIEST WAY TO MAKE FRIENDS OF YOUR LISTENERS

Start with humor.

Doug Lenfesty puts it, "Give them a few laughs."

Do that and the listeners say, "This is going to be different."

And do you know something? We all like a speaker who shows a sense of humor. Show you have that knack and are not afraid to use it and listeners relax. They know this is going to be good, better or best.

HUMOR FIRST, THEN THE SPEECH

That's why you hear so many speeches start with a line like, "I didn't mean to tell you this, but your chairman is my cousin—" The speaker has set you up now and can follow that with, "I got a thousand first cousins but he's the one that wears shoes," or "speaks English," or has some other ridiculous qualification. Then remarks like, "The family down in the hills is mighty proud of Horace. They talk about him a lot particularly about those oil rights he sold them." Listeners like that kind of kidding. Horace likes it too if the speaker has cleared what he will say with him. It indicates that the speaker is not a stuffed shirt. This is a regular Ann or Andy, a person the listener would enjoy knowing.

SHOW YOU WANT TO BE FRIENDS

Humor makes friends and that's why so many speeches start with an anecdote. Here's one I heard last month at a Marketing Club meeting. The speaker said, "I was sitting upstairs in my hotel room studying the notes of this speech. The telephone rang and the man said he was Mr. Nelson from the Club. 'Have a good trip in?' he asked. I said I had. 'Is your room all right?' I admitted it was. He said, 'The meeting room is on the second floor, when you are ready to come down, I'll meet you in the bar and we'll have a drink, ok?' That was the best offer I had and I met him in the bar. We got acquainted, ordered the first drink, talked through that and ordered another. When that was low, Jake Nelson, he was Jake now, urged me to have another, but I held back. I asked, 'Are you an officer of this club?"

"No, I'm not an officer," he admitted.

"Are you chairman of a committee?"

"No, I'm a one-man committee. It's my job to get the speaker organized. We've found that a drink or two helps loosen up a speaker."

"Well, Ladies, Gentlemen, I have been properly loosened up."

He turned to the chairman, pretended to listen, then told the audience, "Your chairman tells me that there are no ladies here. That shows he wonders how well I've been organized. Perhaps when Jake organizes you, you stay organized." All in good fun, all relaxing.

USE THIS "ON THE WAY HERE" IDEA

The vaudeville performer used this device for a starter, "On my way over to the theatre tonight—" The audience waited expectantly for what happened. Today's speaker uses a modern version of this start when he says, "All my life I've been hearing speakers say, "On my way over to this hall tonight, here's what happened.' Now nothing has ever happened to me on the way to a speaking engagement" Pause "until tonight." Now comes the description of the happening.

HOW HUMOR ESTABLISHES RAPPORT

Note how the examples tend to do this—the "cousin" material indicates that the speaker is no high-born character, no big shot, he is up from humble beginnings.

The "organized" story shows that two drinks are enough for the speaker. Most listeners are modest drinkers.

The "ladies and gentlemen" goof demonstrates that the speaker makes mistakes like the rest of us.

All these bits make friends because the listener feels that he too is that kind of person. You need such rapport at the start and all through the speech.

CAN YOU BE HUMOROUS?

Of course you can. Some speakers are humorous without any great effort. Others have to study and practice to learn the art. A young lady student confides, "I just can't be humorous in my speeches." My question is, "You have a sense of humor, don't you?" She begins to doubt, for nobody will admit he is without a sense of humor. But too many are afraid of displaying that sense. My advice is try to put yourself into this world you hesitate to join, be funny, try for laughs. It is not too difficult to get them.

HERE'S HOW ONE LADY DID IT

I served as a judge at a speech contest put on by a Toastmistress Club. One of the contestants was assigned the subject "Frustrations." What did she use for material? She built a story on her suspicion that her husband was trying to educate her in mechanics, so that she could fix the home appliances that get out of whack, and he never seemed to have time to tackle. She thought it was thoughtful when he gave her a screw driver and later a pair of gift-wrapped pliers did not arouse her suspicions too much, but when he gave her an electric drill with all the attachments for Christmas, she got the message. She didn't want to be thought of as a competent service man, she didn't want to be a clinging vine either. She felt that she would be happier at some stage in between. You can imagine the humor the speaker got into this situation. The listeners had fun listening, there were many laughs, and the judges must have thought well of it also because the speaker was voted the first place. Think of the frustrations she might have talked about—food prices, shortages, Congressional inaction—but she got her material out of her home, her family, and her everyday life.

JOE BANKISS SHOWED HE COULD

At a convention in Kansas City I met Joe Bankiss, a young man who had taken my speaking course.

"I've got to make a speech today," he told me, then asked, "Could you listen and tell me if your teaching has helped me?" I agreed to sit through the effort. The speech was well done, and there were laughs all through it. He told a silly story about a kangaroo that went into a bar and ordered a martini. The bartender served the martini. The kangaroo looked at it and asked, "Since when are you serving martinis without an olive?"

The bartender supplied the olive and said, "Pardon me."

The kangaroo drank his martini, paid for it, and departed.

A customer who had watched the encounter told the bartender, "That is the strangest thing I've ever seen in a bar."

The bartender agreed, "It sure is. I've been tending bar for thirty years and that's the first time I ever forgot to put an olive in a martini."

The customer ordered a refill. When the bartender returned with it, he said, "By rights, Mister, if he wanted an olive he should have asked for it."

His joke ended with the "first time in thirty years" but he gave the story an extra line because he wanted to make the point "If you want something, you have to ask for it." In addition to this story, this speaker used a number of cracks, short one-line pieces that got laughs. Ones I made notes of were—"home is where you can trust the hash," and "the boss is a modest man because he's got a lot to be modest about."

When I met Joe later, I said, "You're one of the fellows who insisted you couldn't be humorous. How come all those laughs?"

"You told me I could be funny, didn't you?"

I admitted my guilt.

"I didn't believe you," he said, "but as I studied what made for humor in speeches, I began to think maybe you were right. I tried some of the ideas that others used, and the listeners laughed. I think those laughs make it easier for them to do the serious parts—looking for that next gag, maybe, but listening to the meat and potatoes also."

THIS PLAN WILL WORK FOR YOU

Note these steps:

First, study what gets laughs for others. Chapter 3 shows you how to do that, and

Second, try using the same kind of material. Joe found it worked for him. You'll find it works for you.

TRY AND YOU'LL SUCCEED

You may say, "I'm no good at telling gags and stories." Change that to, "I'll get good." All you need is observation, practice, and persistence. Maybe your first tries will not be what you want, but keep trying. You'll improve. The effort will pay off because humor does so much for a speaker—

it projects a picture of a friendly person
it promises enjoyment for the listeners, and
it builds a togetherness between speaker and listeners,
and, as Joe Bankiss told me, "They listen better."

2

CASH IN ON WHAT HAPPENS TO YOU

You are your funniest speech subject.

Yes, I mean you.

Let's say you start by admitting, "I had a hunch this day was not going to be one of my best. I like to get out of bed on the right side; I feel that if I get out the right side my day starts right. But this morning–"

You got attention with that start. There is a hint of humor in what you have said. And all ears are tuned to see why and how you fouled up.

HUMOR IS ALL AROUND YOU

A woman in my speech class said, "I couldn't talk about the silly gifts my husband gives me, or our little family squabbles. I'd be too embarrassed and he wouldn't like it either." If you have such an attitude, you miss many opportunities for humor or eloquence. Most speakers get out a joke book, or ask friends if they have heard a good story that they can use. And the things that happen to them every day can furnish most of the humor they need. Check this the next time you listen to a speech. What do the listeners laugh at? Isn't the speaker's report on things like–

- his big ideas that didn't work
- his alibi that didn't convince
- his explanation that didn't explain
- the time the big bruiser threatened to clobber him
- or the sweet young thing that called him "Grandad."

Of course, listeners laugh at the gag stories or the night club jokes if you can tell them well. But stories of your own experiences are better for you. You can't forget the action. You were there. You did this, said this. The other did this, said this. Here's one such incident I use in a speech–

LOOK FOR THIS KIND OF HUMOR

I was working on the front lawn the other day when a young fellow about eight or nine years of age came down the sidewalk. He was followed by a rope and a brown dog with floppy ears. The rope was tied around the dog's neck and was held by the boy. I greeted him, "Hi, there, young man."

He asked, "Want to buy a dog?"

I asked, "Why should I buy that dog?"

The boy said, "He's a good dog. He's house broke. He minds well. He does tricks. Don't you, Samson?" He looked at the dog and I'd swear that Samson nodded his head.

I asked, "Does he have a pedigree?"

"You don't have to worry about that. We had him to the vet to be fixed and he's been fine ever since."

You may ask, "You call that stuff speech material?" I can testify that it is the kind that most good speakers use. Analyze it–a story–characters, a man, a boy and a dog–conversation–struggle–some doubt of the outcome and it is amusing.

All that in less than one minute. The listener is urging, "Go on, tell me more." Such a story can be developed to make most points you want to make.

WHY THIS KIND OF EXCHANGE HOLDS ATTENTION

It could happen to anybody. Suppose it happened to you and you told about it? You know others would listen, perhaps ask questions. Well, listeners are much like that person at the next desk. And think how easy the speaker got it! The incident walked into his life. Listeners can imagine it walking into their lives.

REMEMBER ALL OF US FUMBLE

Listeners relate to your misadventures. They remember when they tried to help and got bawled out by the one they were trying to assist. Your story on your adventure that brought embarrassment to you shows that you too blunder. They laugh at your frustration. They say, "Welcome to the club." They understand how innocent third parties can get into such troubles and they don't downrate you for it. With most of them life is just one setback after another. They mean well, but–. Of course the experienced speaker uses standard jokes that are found in his joke book. But most speech humor comes from adventures in the speaker's own wonderland.

YOUR BIG MOUTH IS MIGHTY HELPFUL

Most occurrences that get laughs are connected with your big mouth. You opened it, said something, and somebody thought you meant something else. Listeners know how that is. They have opened their mouths to say the wrong thing at the wrong time and they know that they would have saved trouble if they had remained a part of the silent majority.

LAUGH AT YOUR FAVORITE CLOWN

You may say, "Those goofs of mine aren't funny to me." Maybe so, but if you are the kind that doesn't laugh at your own clumsiness, you are never going to be a humorous speaker. Accept my assurance that listeners will laugh at your accounts of your fumblings. Will Rogers said, "Anything is funny if it happens to the other person." When you are speaking, you are the other person to the audience. Listen to the funny stories that speakers tell and you'll be surprised at the high percentage that bring laughs on the speaker. The man reports his wife tells him to shape up, his kids show him no respect, his small grandson spills Grandad's hair dye on the yellow bathroom rug. And he was trying to keep that dye hidden from his wife. The woman speaker reports how she misread the recipe and got too much of one ingredient in the stew. She reports her husband ate some and said that he wasn't very hungry tonight. The kids' remarks indicated the operation of one happy family. The little one asked, "Did you learn to make this in cooking school, Mommy?" The speakers report the mishaps with a smile. And you like them better for it.

HOW OTHERS HELP YOU

Think of how many times you laugh during the day, at little things that occur in your daily routine—conversations with your boss, associates, employees, friends, bus drivers, bartenders, your wife, kids, relatives, all people you contact without going out of your way. Your day is full of humorous adventures. You'll see something, read something, experience something and you'll get the idea that perhaps you can develop the item and use it as speech material.

YOUR FRUSTRATIONS SCORE WELL

Let's say you asked your secretary to go down to the machine on the floor below and get you a package of cigarettes. She says, "Smoking cigarettes is dangerous to your health and I refuse to help shorten anybody's life." As you walk down to the cigarette machine you think over that remark. See any humor in it? If you told the boss he might say, "She's right, you smoke too much," or, "Think we should pay a girl one hundred fifty bucks a week to go for cigarettes?" Already I'll bet you have thought of other complications. For instance, the cigarette machine took your coins but didn't work. You pressed the coin-return button but no coins came back. You called the office manager and she told you you were not supposed to use that machine, it was for the sole use of the top executives. Now you explode, the system is working at its usual efficiency. But you have yourself covered with humor. Listeners sympathize, but they laugh at a boss who thinks he should be treated as one of the high and mighty.

This chain of events demonstrates how to build up any happening. Let your imagination run wild, and you'll come up with an account that causes listeners to laugh at the expert who is reduced to a sad sack, by the same kind of rules and accidents that frustrate them.

DIGNITY DOESN'T PAY SO WELL

One of the fallacious ideas is that speakers have to be dignified, that they shouldn't unbend or let themselves go. But what a difference when they do unbend. The statesman appearing on a TV program reads his opening statement with dignity that indicates his importance, stately words, dignified phrasing, modulated voice. Then one of the reporters asks a question that irritates the great man. Now his hair falls out of place and he digs into his tormentor. You like the great man better when he forgets he is a Poobah. Listeners like you better when you show you are like them. Be yourself, tell things as they happened, let yourself go. Tell about the argument you had with your spouse last week. It may be history as far as family relations go, but it makes excellent speech material.

Think about humor material for your speeches this way:

1. Your experiences are funnier than any printed material you can find. Always picture yourself as the butt of the joke.
2. Jokes you read can be improved by putting yourself in them, always as the fall guy.
3. Tell about any experience many times before you try to use it in a speech. Practice telling it to the wife and kids, the boys at the office.

LAUGH AT YOURSELF AND YOU RATE HIGHER

There are three kinds of laughter–

1. The humorist who laughs at his own jokes. You know him–the fellow who is always reporting the wisecrack he made to the traffic cop or the fellow worker. Listeners may laugh at this type, but he rates low with them.
2. The laughter of those who laugh at the jokes of others–you would love to have many of these in your audiences.
3. The laughter of the man who laughs at himself. This is the highest form of humor. Psychologists tell you, "When you laugh at yourself, you indicate you can look at yourself objectively." But your interest in laughs on yourself comes because this is the kind of laughter that listeners appreciate most. Show you can laugh at yourself, even though you are the biggest of the big, and the listeners welcome you to their club.

3

HOW TO MAKE LISTENERS LAUGH

Listen to speakers who make listeners laugh, and you'll find that they use the same subjects. One is a wife slanderer, another tells of his in-laws, a third explains his inability to communicate with his kids. In each case he comes out second best. The woman speaker uses her home duties or the office routine to help her. One attempts to tell of her efforts to be a good cook and she finds the packaged foods they offer today burn too easily or the frozen food makers don't recommend enough time to cook the stuff. Another explains how she tried to go along with the women's libbers and what happened to her; a third talks about her brother-in-law who is the superior *man.* Both women and men can dig into the people that work with them—the boss, the other managers and their associates. Some humor you hear is far out, but most of it concerns the lives the speakers live every day.

SUBJECTS THAT GO OVER BEST

I checked through my notes of humorous items that I have heard speakers use and came up with these–

Family: husband-wife–in-laws–small children–teenagers–

News of day: a speaker said this–

Fads, foibles: exercises–diets–women's lib–

Pets: the dog that insists on camping in your easy chair–the cat that chases butterflies–the parakeet that won't talk–

Sports: the games we watch and play–

On-the-job: the boss–the secretaries–the associates–

Characters we all know: bus drivers–bartenders–taxi drivers–panhandlers–

Advertisers: print and TV–making fun of them makes laugh material–

JUST LIVE YOUR LIFE

You have experiences in all of those areas and should be able to come up with items in many of them. The advantage of using this type of humor is that you are a part of it, even if it is only as an observer. If in your account of the experience, you say nothing or do nothing, listners can picture your doing just that. If you open your mouth and get into trouble, they can figure that, too.

THE IDEAS THAT BRING LAUGHS

These run the whole scale of what is funny. For instance–

Nonsense–the farmer told by his banker that he has a good wife agrees with, "Yes, she is. I wish I had a few more like her." The kangaroo ordering the martini comes in this classification.

Surprise–unexpected–the speaker says, "Here you sit listening to a good speech by a good speaker."

Truth–the speaker cracks, "It's better to have halitosis than no breath at all."

The Ridiculous–the high school boy tells his dad that they are working on a solution that will dissolve anything. The dad asks, "What are you going to hold it in?" The boy answers,"We'll work on that later."

The Incongruous–the fellow studying the racing form in church.

Big Words–a man in the meeting asks, "How many of you attending this meeting are extroverts?" The chairman answers, "I don't know about the rest but I'm a Democrat." The wife excuses the husband who always looks like a tramp with, "He likes to dress casual." The shoeshine boy says, "I hesitate to respond." *Note:* The big word must be one most listeners know.

Ad-Libs–These at least bring smiles, but they call for care in handling. "He is a master mortician–he went to school in Chicago to learn how to look sad at a ten thousand dollar funeral." Most such ad-libs should be rehearsed.

Asides–A fact is stated, then a humorous thought. (This fellow's name is Al Samson. Al was allergic to work. (Fact.) (This fault ran in his family. (Aside.)

Insults–TV comedians use this form, but I advise against it if you don't make a living out of comedy. Sarcasm or the cutting remark may turn off the listeners. Lay off your wife and her relatives unless you come out second best in your encounters with them.

Irony–watch it. The fatso may not like being called "Slim" or the slim one "Fatso."

Exaggeration–As a boy I heard the line, "A covey of quail flew out of his beard." We saw lots of beards in those days. Last week I heard, "The car backfired and a covey of sparrows flew out of his beard." Beards are back now. Another–"The burglar got religion and brought back everything he stole from our house plus a lot of things he got somewhere else."

Similes–You say, "He got out of there fast like–" Don't use familiar ones like "a cat on a hot tin roof." Try to make up one that is your original.

Other Types—you hear daffynitions—usually good for a smile—an expert is anybody away from home with a brief case—mutilated quotations—a penny saved is a penny earned—if your wife doesn't find out—the play on words—the ice cream commercial that urges, "Give her a brick for Mother's Day."

You may think of a type of humor not listed. But any one of the ones mentioned can bring laughs for you.

STORIES AND ONE-LINERS

A story that takes a few minutes to tell may be enough to get a laugh by itself. It would get a stronger laugh if it were told after other stories. If you tell one story the listener may not get the idea that he is supposed to laugh. Tell two and he begins to catch on. Tell three and he understands.

YOU'RE LUCKY IN THE GREAT AMOUNT OF LAUGH MATERIAL AVAILABLE

A study of the list of subjects and ideas that have always made listeners laugh should convince you that you *don't* need—

1. The night club saloon type joke about the movie star's drinking, the comedian's stinginess, the starlet's ample endowment. This type suggests an intimacy that you perhaps can't claim.
2. Off-color jokes that can only help picture you as a low-brow.
3. Stories you hear on TV. The listener has probably heard this one too. And the man on TV probably can tell it better than you do.
4. To worry about humor to use, the supply seems to be unending.

4

HUMOR CAN HELP OR HARM

Humor is not an asset in every speech. Speakers tell me, "Ed, I have to make a speech. Give me a couple of gags or stories to tell." I ask, what is your subject, who is the audience, and a few other questions to spark their thinking on whether or not they need humor. In most cases the questions do not bother them–they want to be comedians.

Before you decide on using humor, consider these points:

THE PROS AND CONS OF USING HUMOR

First, let's look at those rare cases when humor may not be needed.

1. *It May Not Fit:* The subject is so serious to the group that it is risky to laugh at it. The points for or against are so important that the story about Aunt Minny and the TV man may be out of place.

2. *An Overdose May Give the Wrong Impression:* The listener may feel the speaker is too frivolous. This is a common fault with business speakers. The salesman laughs at the product, the advertising manager at the advertisement. They try for the laugh when a bit of reason-why talk or a demonstration would be more effective. You see this in TV commercials. The laugh at the end of the commercial may obscure the list of benefits presented earlier.
3. *Some Laughs Are in Bad Taste:* The laugh may lead the listeners to think the speaker has poor taste. The crack about the dumb ethnic may seem hilarious to the speaker, but it may antagonize an audience even if they are not of the same breed. If the speaker belittles one group of ethnics, listeners may wonder how he feels about their group.
4. *The Listeners May Not Get the Point:* Nothing makes a speaker look worse than a gag that listeners don't understand and explanations make it look worse. Most comedians have lines to use in such cases that tell the listener, "You should have laughed." But the inexperienced speaker just flounders on. There is no sense in repeating the gag.
5. *The Speaker May Be Inept:* I have said that any speaker can be funny, but some of them won't take the time to learn how to handle stories and gags. You have heard speakers forget the gag lines in their stories. Listeners feel sorry for them. Remember any speaker who is funny practiced and rehearsed. A woman speaker told me, "I think being a clown detracts from the dignity of the speaker." With that attitude it would be difficult for her to use humor as effectively as the speaker who goes all out for the laugh.
6. *Competition Is Tough:* The speaker who tries for humor is competing with the professionals on TV. Those people have studied the art, and they can be expected to do better than any part-time humorist. Listeners are certain to compare the speaker with skilled performers.
7. *The Laugh Leads the Speaker on a Detour:* A laugh or a bit of applause has an electrifying effect on a speaker. Listeners laugh and the speaker's common sense flies out the window.

The success with the first laugh increases the speaker's need for more laughs, more applause.

WHY HUMOR IS HELPFUL

I have mentioned three reasons why it helps to use humor—

1. Listeners Like It.
2. It Is Expected, and
3. It Gives a Better Impression of the Speaker.

Here are some other benefits—

4. *It Relaxes:* The warm up before the variety shows on TV was to get the audience laughing before the show started so that the mood would carry over into the show. The speaker who starts the speech with a laugh or two finds it easier to get the group to laugh at gags that come later. Listeners would rather laugh than try to figure out what you mean by a serious statement. The speaker who laughs with his listeners loses some of his tenseness.
5. *Softens the Dull and Tiresome:* The material may not be dull to the speaker, but it may be to a large percentage of the listeners. How many times have you wished for a button or switch that would turn off a speaker. The subject didn't interest you and the speaker didn't interest you. You knew what was wanted and so the speech was finished but the speaker yakked on and on. When a speaker with a dull subject introduces some wit, a wisecrack, or a funny story, your attention is intensified. You feel the humor is an attempt to ease your problem in listening to his dull subject.
6. *Brings Back Attention:* The speaker who loses attention with his dull subject can be assured of recapturing that attention with the magic words, "Once upon a time—" If a short bit gets a laugh, those about to go to sleep snap to attention. Another shortie or two and listeners are listening again.

LET YOUR HUMOR HELP MAKE POINTS

Humor can contribute to your talk in the ways listed. But why not let it contribute more than a laugh. One gag may contribute only a laugh. Another can contribute the laugh plus a point that helps further your objective. Try to make your selections do those two jobs. They may laugh at your account of your repeated attempts to get the approval of the boss. But when you report you got it on the fifth try, you can make your point, "Isn't that how most of us are? We go off half prepared, when with a bit of thought we could have prepared properly and got the approval the first time?"

Another point you might have made with this advice is—"That's something we seldom do—try five times. We try once, maybe twice and quit. If I had quit after two attempts, I would have failed. But I believed and kept trying. That's how we have to tackle this problem, try once, twice, three times and keep trying until we get the job done.

HOW TO MAKE POINTS WITH GAGS

I heard an office manager make a point on planning with a clever bit that was mighty funny to me. She thought she needed some relief in the talk and used this bit,

"The movie star married four times but she had a life plan in mind. Listen to this—her first husband was a banker, her second was a movie producer, her third a beautician, and her fourth an undertaker. Where's the plan in that you ask? OK, how about this—One for the money, two for the show, three to get ready and four to go? It's a plan, isn't it?" The story got a big laugh for her, and gave her a break before she got down to the nitty gritty of how each of her workers could use more planning.

MAKE NOTES OF POSSIBLE POINTS

Remember this point-making idea when you make a note of a remark, an incident or gag or story that you might use. Let your notes cover the gag and the point you might make with it. For instance, let's assume you read this joke in your morning newspaper—

A wife asks her husband—

"Did anyone ever tell you how romantic, how handsome, how fascinating you are?"

He says, "Why no, dear, I don't think anyone ever did."

She asks, "Well, where did you ever get the idea?"

This is a conversation that might take place in any household. If you think it funny, try to figure out what points you can make with it. How about these points that I have emphasized with this bit–

We don't see ourselves as others see us.

We don't act our age.

Our wives are smarter than we are.

A man can dream, can't he?

From such a gag you can perhaps figure other points. I can testify that my selections worked well for me.

TO USE OR NOT TO USE

There will be mighty few occasions when humor is not welcome. Some listeners laugh when the humor is in bad taste or does not fit the subject or the occasion. This proves the popularity of humor. To be safe, follow these thoughts:

1. When it is not apropos, forget it.
2. Use enough to give the listeners the impression that you are a person they would like to follow, claim relationship to, do business with.
3. Get double duty out of your humor by having it help you make points.

5

HAVE FUN FINDING LAUGH MATERIAL

Humor is everywhere.

You can't get away from it.

Think how tough the daily grind would be if it wasn't relieved by the flashes of humor that interrupt the even tenor of the day. I say—

- read all humor
- listen to it
- make notes of what you think funny
- be receptive to it and you'll find more than any one speaker can use.

WHERE TO FIND HUMOROUS MATERIAL

I have mentioned your daily experiences at home, at the office, moving about, playing or watching your favorite sport. Then think of these sources—

Newspapers

Many feature a bit called "Laugh for the Day." The cartoons have many ideas to offer. Even the strip cartoons which carry the adventures of the characters from day to day will give you ideas. A good source is the one picture cartoons. They present an idea that is supposed to bring a laugh.

Magazines

Get the habit of reading through the columns that claim to be funny. Give each thought enough time in trying to see the humor. Many trade papers have a column or page of bright sayings.

Joke Books

I must have fifty of these books bought over the years, hard cover and paperback, with thousands of stories and gags that someone has collected for my use. Some have the subjects of the jokes indexed to make it easier to find a joke that fits your subject. The authors may call them anthologies, encyclopedias, manuals. Think of them as help.

SOME NOT FUNNY TO YOU

In studying any humorous material in print, you'll find some offerings that don't seem funny to you. They are like the cracks of the comedians on TV that you don't quite hear. Don't waste time trying to figure them out. You'll find many that you think good.

HOW TO BUILD A FILE OF HUMOR FOR SPEECHES

1. *Read and Listen:* Follow the comedy sources in your newspaper and magazines, the columns, the jokes, the cartoons. The other day a young lady asked me, "I never look at the cartoons. Does that make me more adult?" I can't answer that question about the adult part, but I know that she is missing a lot of speech material. Listen to the comedians on radio and TV and to the people around you.

2. *Make Notes of Incidents That Amuse You:* When a gag, a story or a remark at lunch gets a laugh, make a note of it. You

may say, "I'm not good at remembering such things." Take heart, nobody is. Your note of the bit can assist your memory. Make your note complete enough to bring back the whole gag or story. If it's a gag, write it out completely. If it is a story, write out enough so that you lose none of the idea.

3. *File the Joke Only If You Think It Is Funny:* You won't think every humorous bit you read or hear is funny. I read and hear perhaps 25 gags and stories each week. Perhaps one or two out of the lot strike me as being worthy of noting. I have a large file with hundreds of these notes. Later when I refer to some of the notes, I wonder why I thought the piece had possibilities. Use only those stories or gags you think funny. If they don't seem funny to you, you will not make them sound funny to others.

4. *Put Yourself into the Story:* When you have a story about a mishap to your neighbor, change the characters and have that mishap happen to you. The listener can see you and you don't have to waste words describing your main character. Maybe the neighbor's teenager made the funny remark to his dad. If possible, have your teenage hopeful make it to you. If you can put yourself into the story, you'll find it goes better.

5. *Let the Other Be the Hero:* Perhaps your remark did devastate the crook who was trying to put something over on you, but let somebody else make the remark. If the gag is the kind that makes you the smart one, forget that version, give the smart line to another character. Here's how–Let's say I made the remark that turned down the crook. In telling the story it would help if I indicated that I was about to go for the gold brick. The crook had me sold completely. I was all ready to buy. I called in my secretary, let her hear his story and she made the crack that confounded the slicker. Maybe I got some credit for hiring such a smart secretary, but I made her the heroine and kept myself a character that listeners had a better chance of liking.

6. *Use Modern Characters:* In your stories use people the listener knows, the bus driver, the elevator starter, office manager, your secretary, the gang at the Last Chance Bar and Grill. Listeners will feel at home with such characters. The knight in his clanking armor isn't as familiar as the woman next

door testifying for Cold Power or the fellow at the next desk showing the new shoes he bought at Penney's.

7. *Keep Within the Listener's Knowledge:* Use places they know. Actions they understand. When you tell about the lecture the cop gave you in addition to a ticket, the listener isn't confused. Think of the life you live every day and try to stay within those limits. Keep talking about air flights when the listeners seldom ride a plane and they may think you are trying to impress them.

8. *Make It Fit the Times:* The best response comes from humor that fits the times. Stories in old joke books feature a number of gags about old maids, boarding houses, train travel. Today that might have to be changed to woman's lib, fast food spots, and auto trips. At one time the fact that a character's coat and pants didn't match might indicate that he was not too prosperous. Today some of the most prosperous don't have one outfit of matching coat and pants.

9. *Think of Variety:* Use a variety of characters and locales for your stories you plan to use in one speech. If everything seems to happen in the one place, you may give the wrong impression. In one speech I told three stories about happenings in bars and grills. Later one listener asked me, "You drink very much?" I should have put one incident in church, one at the office, the other in the bar. Now when I tell a story about a bit of dialogue in a bar, I usually explain I went in to use the telephone. Listeners laugh at that and say, "Oh, yeah?" But they don't rate me as a lush.

10. *Avoid Dialect:* Most speakers are not too good at it. If you think you are good at one dialect, and use it, you may offend someone. In most instances the story is just as funny in the vernacular you use every day. If it is not funny without dialect, forget the story.

11. *Rehearse Any Gag or Story:* Tell your funny story to your spouse, the neighbor at the next desk, the gang at lunch. Tell it again to the brother-in-law when he comes over to borrow the ice cubes. If they laugh, the story may have possibilities. If they don't understand, perhaps you better not try the story. Telling

it to friends gives you rehearsal and practice. Surely, you know the story, but practice helps you tell it better.

12. *Try to Visualize Your Characters:* As you tell a story think of the character you are telling about. Your car did slide into the other fellow's car. The damage was a scratch on his rear fender that was difficult to see. But the character tried to make a major repair job out of it. You lived through the incident, didn't you? You have a good picture of this character shouting, gesturing, reviling, browbeating a helpless woman. Well, think of that picture and try to pass it on to the hearers. Your story is only as good as the characters who come to life in it.

13. *Protect Your Material:* You may have a story that gets a big laugh for you. You may find that the speaker ahead of you at the meeting uses your gem. I once had that happen to me and I got a better laugh by telling the listeners, "The speaker who spoke before me used one of my stories, but since I tell it better than he does, I'm going to use it again." The story was important in emphasizing a point. I needed it at that spot in the speech. It pays to protect your material. An associate asks, "Can I use your donkey story in this meeting? It gets such a big laugh." Tell him, "I'd rather you didn't. Let's look through my file for one that would go better for you."

14. *Forget Failures:* If a story you tell falls flat, don't pause as if you are puzzled. Keep on talking. The story was a bit of decoration. The next story you tell may go over big. A comedian makes his living on laughs and he has to fight for laughs. But as a speaker you can tell yourself, "I have my first objective—and it's not to be funny."

15. *Find and File:* The story or gag you hear today may be lost to you forever if you do nothing about it. Make a note of the idea and you will be able to remember it and use it in the future. Follow this plan—

a. Make notes of ideas you think humorous, and
b. File them in a way that is convenient for you
c. If you don't think the gag that gets a laugh is funny, forget it. If you don't think it is humorous, you won't be able to tell it in a way that gets others to laugh.

6

HOW TO EDIT HUMOROUS MATERIAL FOR SPEAKING

The stories and jokes you read in print were written for printing. In writing none of us use the same words we do in speaking. And so the joke writer may have used words you would never use in speaking. If you try to tell the joke in words you never speak, you may have trouble saying the words and pronouncing them correctly. In addition, words you don't use regularly may be difficult to remember. Before you use any story or gag you get from a printed page, go over it and change the wording to fit your speaking vocabulary. Think of these places to check:

1. *Use "He Said" and "She Said":* In the stories you read you will find descriptive words to indicate how the character spoke–demurred–stated–explained–admonished–exclaimed–

parroted–objected. Change all of these to "said." Do the same with answered–replied–argued–and other such descriptions. "Said" is easier to hear than any of the more exact descriptions.

2. *Eliminate Descriptions of How the Character Said It:* Change such lines as, "She said in a disdainful voice," to, "She said." Let the way you speak the line show the disdain. You need no description of the mood of the character who says, "Go jump in the lake," "Is that so?" or "You and who else?" You can't make such remarks without indicating you want to fight.

3. *Make Conversation True to Life:* Don't report a character in your story as using a word like "desist." The person would probably sound more natural saying, "Stop it," or "Cut that." If your character is a learned type that might use "desist," leave it as is. This may add to the comedy, for one of the sources of humor are those words the learned use with the not-so-learned. Most laugh lines do not need impressive words. For instance, the woman answering the telephone asks, "Whom do you want?" The caller says, "I got the wrong number." The woman asks, "How do you know you got the wrong number?" He says, "I don't know anybody who says 'whom.' "

4. *Check Out Words You Never Speak:* Find a word to substitute for any word you might not normally use or that might not be familiar to your listener. Don't allow a character to say "unilateral" when he means "one-sided." In descriptions of action follow this practice with fairly simple words. Change "he resided in Hoboken" to the more familiar "he lived in Hoboken." Listeners would hear the word "resided," but "lived" is the word most of them would use. Instead of "classmate" use "in my class." On one printed page in a story collection I found these words, engrossed–belligerent–chuckling–unflappable–escorting. You can substitute simpler words for every one of those, can't you? The simpler word is easier to hear and understand.

HOW TO IMPROVE THE LAUGH LINE

Your humor is of little use if it doesn't bring the laugh, the smile or the chuckle you intended. And many times a joke fails because the speaker hasn't given enough thought to that laugh line. These tips apply to the two types of humor that are used most often by speakers.

5. *Cut the Number of Words:* It is easier to remember and say a laugh line of a few words. It is easier for the listener to hear. Prove this to yourself by trying to read a long headline in your newspaper to your spouse. No matter how carefully you read it, you'll hear, "What did you say?" There would be no question if the headline was, "Drop dead."

6. *How to Make the Laugh Line Easier to Hear:* If the laugh line is long, try breaking it into two sentences. Here is an example–suppose the line is, "There is no better way to bridge the gap between strangers than a laugh." The line counts to 14 words. That would speak better as, "A laugh is the best way to bridge the gap between strangers." It will speak even better in two questions, thus–"What's the best way to bridge the gap between strangers?" *(Pause)* "Isn't it a laugh?"

A BIT OF CREATIVITY MAKES THE STORY YOURS

Any change you make in the story, the characters or the laugh line helps make it your own story. You found what you thought was a good story in a magazine. You thought it would go better if you changed it a bit and so you made the change–the two plumbers became two M.D.'s–by changing a few words. Now you'll tell the story about the two M.D's with more confidence. Once you start revising anecdotes for speaking you'll find you have more creative ability than you suspected. One speaker told me, "That's not creativity, that's courage or is it plagiarism?" Call it what you prefer, but by changing a bit of action, a character, or a few words, the gag becomes yours. You'll find that stories you have worked on in this way go better for you.

THESE STEPS MAKE YOU A BETTER LAUGH PRODUCER

a. Use only words you would normally use in any humor you attempt.

b. Revise the laugh line so that it is easier to say. That will make it easier to hear.

c. Change characters to ones the listeners might know—traffic cops, bus drivers, taxi drivers, waitresses, bosses, secretaries, and such like. Oh, yes, ministers, priests and bishops are ok, too.

7

PLANNING HELPS GET BIGGER LAUGHS

A listener will not smile or laugh at your humor if he doesn't–

- hear it, or
- understand it.

SPEAK LOUD ENOUGH, SLOW ENOUGH AND DISTINCTLY

Every evening listening to TV, wives and husbands ask their mates, "What did he say?" And the mate's answer, "I didn't hear it." The speaker had rushed the remark, mumbled it, or, as they say in the trade, "threw it away." The mechanical applause machine produced loud laughs at the gag but mighty few of the listeners had. Both the speaker and listeners lost. To prevent this happening to you–

REHEARSE THAT LAUGH LINE

Last week I heard a speaker make this crack, "A dropout, eh? A scholar slip." He had to be careful pronouncing that last word, or most of the listeners would hear "scholarship." They would ask, "What's funny about that?" Watch comedians on TV and you'll find that many performers speak a bit slower and louder when they speak the laugh line. The gags you miss are either rushed or mumbled. Plan to avoid this too common fault–speak up, speak slowly and enunciate clearly. One way to do this is to set the laugh line apart, think of it as a separate part of the speech. Rehearse saying it–louder, slowly, and speak each word distinctly.

Master the Pause: The pause is a great help in insuring the laugh line gets its laugh or at least a smile. The pause draws the listeners' attention back to you, it gives listeners time to hear and understand. In the example I gave earlier here is how a pause can be used–"A drop out, eh?" *(Pause)* "A scholar slip?" Good gagsters have learned to rely on the *Pause* to help save the laugh for them.

Spotlight the Laugh Line: Set it apart. Use any device to help the listener hear and understand what you say. Let's say the laugh line is, "Drop dead." This is short, perhaps too short. Its saving grace is that it is familiar, and would be heard. Too many laugh lines are in language not so familiar. Care is needed to make sure that listeners know what the speaker said. With a short line, I use a question before the pause. The question is, "Do you know what this girl said?" Now a pause while listeners try to figure out what was said. Then I continue, "She said," *Pause,* " 'Drop dead.' " The question gives the listener a problem. The pause gives him some time to try to answer the question. Then when the laugh line comes loud and clear, he hears it, understands it, and laughs.

THREE GAGS IN A ROW HELP

A listener needs to be prepared to laugh. One short gag hits him cold. You can be on with your speech before he understands he is supposed to laugh. When you want a laugh, don't depend too heavily on one gag, use three in a row. Here's how I use this device in one of my speeches:

I state, "You can improve. I'm mighty optimistic about that. I'll tell you the kind of optimist I am—when I look at a bottle, I don't say, 'It's half empty.' No, I say, 'It's half full.' " *Pause.* I also admit I'm not as full of optimism as the fellow who says, 'It's better to have halitosis than no breath at all,' *Pause,* or the neighbor who insists that he will not admit he is henpecked until he has to wash and iron his own aprons." *Pause.* "But I go overboard in my optimism about you being able to improve."

The first gag gives some listeners the idea that they are supposed to laugh. The second tells others, "This speaker is trying to be funny." The third convinces most you want them to laugh. The first gets to some, the second to more, and the third to most.

THE RULE OF THREE IMPROVES MOST STORIES

If your laugh-producing story is one of the longer ones, use three incidents, three confrontations, three whatevers. The young man asks his little sister, then his mother, then his father. The executive asks his secretary, then an associate, then his boss. Let's say you are a store manager and you are asked to speak to a group of other store managers. You confess it has always bugged you that so many customers came into your store frowning. You know they have a problem, but you have a group of well-trained sales people who can help them solve it. Then why are they frowning? You feel that if a customer is in the best mood to buy, she doesn't have a frown on her face. "What should she have?" you ask.

"A smile," someone suggests.

"Okay, how can we produce that smile?" you go on. "I figured that if I bought a small parakeet, taught it to say, 'What a beautiful smile,' put it on a stand by the front door, I'd get rid of most of those frowns."

"It took me three months to teach the dumb bird to say that line, but I got it perfect at it. The customer came in with her frown, the bird said its piece, and you know what the customer did? She looked at the little bird and smiled. Every sales person said it was a good idea and the customers were in better humor. Other merchants came to see how it worked. I felt so good about it I thought of calling up one of the trade magazine editors and telling him about my success. So far, so good, but Tuesday morning I cut myself shaving. I had to get the cut patched up, then hurrying, I slipped and fell in the shower. Next, in a rush to get to work on time a traffic light on the boulevard changed too fast and I got a ticket. You can imagine my mood when I arrived at the store. I opened the front door and that dumb bird said, 'What a beautiful smile.' Right then I exploded. I turned to the bird and shouted, 'Can't you say anything but *What a beautiful smile?*' The minute I said it I was sorry. The bird looked hurt, dejected. I was about to apologize when it piped up, 'Boss, what do you think I am? A genius?' "

NOTE THE THREES

The store owner had to buy the bird, teach him to say the words, stand him on the perch by the front door. The narrator cuts himself shaving, falls in the shower, gets a ticket. After you have heard of these mishaps, you can see why he is in a mood to scream at the bird of good cheer.

Note how the rule of three is used in many ways through the following story:

Late one night Murphy, Kelly and Clancy were staggering home from choir practice singing at the top of their voices. They came to Clancy's house. One of them started knocking on the front door. That brought no response so another started to help with the knocking. Still no response. Then all three of them started pounding. A window upstairs opened. A voice yelled, "Get out of here you bums before I call the cops."

"We can't leave until you come down here and help us, Mrs. Clancy," one of the men called.

"Why do you need help?"

"Somebody's got to tell us which is Clancy."

"Who cares?"

"We do."

"Why do you care?"

"The rest of us want to go home."

Note the threes–three characters–three knockers on the door–three bits of conversation.

The threes help the story bring laughs.

THREE HAPPENINGS BUILD UP YOUR LAUGH

The late Max Droke, an authority on humor, called this rule of three "perhaps the most important single principle in the construction of humorous situations." If you have two gags, look for another–a third. As you revise stories from printed material for telling, think of this rule. If you have two happenings in the story, try to think of a third and note how it helps. If you have four instances, cut one and see if the story doesn't tell better.

BUILD-UP HELPS THE PRESENTATION

In using the rule of three let the three things build up. First a small trouble, then a larger trouble, then the largest of the three. You cut yourself shaving, that could happen to any of us and is not too serious, the fall in the shower is more serious, but the ticket, that's bigger trouble. Follow this same idea with gags, use the good one first, the better one next, and the best last. If they laugh at the first, fine, hit them with the second and they laugh a bit louder. Now they are set up for the third to slay them.

USE THESE TRICKS OF THE HUMOROUS SPEAKERS

Think of the line that is supposed to make the listeners laugh as the most important words you use. Study it and practice it. Follow this plan–

1. Speak the words loud enough, slowly, and distinctly.
2. Give the laugh line importance by pausing before you say it.
3. Focus attention on it with a question, such as, "You know what that lady said–"
4. Use three gags or three happenings in your stories. Plan to have your laughs build up–the good first, the better next, and the best last.

Humor is a mighty valuable speaking tool. It may seem that a speaker you hear is naturally humorous. But a check will prove to you that even the funniest work at it. The volume of laughs produced usually are in proportion to the work that went into the breakdown of the material. If you laughed till it hurt at a speaker, he prepared.

Part Two

HOW TO MAKE YOUR ELOQUENCE PAY OFF

I ask students of public speaking, "What is eloquence?"

The answers I get go something like–

"A fire built under the speaker," or,

"A pin stuck in him or her."

The dictionary says eloquence is–"speech that stirs the feelings"–"persuasive and fluent discourse"–"a flow of speech with grace and force."

When I ask, "Can you be eloquent?" the answer is something like, "I suppose, if I get steamed up enough."

Note the three factors in the definitions–your feelings, your words, and the listener's feelings. Some joker will always say, "You should have heard me when I stepped on my kid's skate board and wound up in the basement."

He was eloquent then, he thought. At times we are all eloquent. On other occasions we may need that fire under us, the pin stuck in us, or a subject we feel strongly about.

The chapters in this part of the book will demonstrate how to be eloquent in feeling, in the words you use, and in arousing the feeling of your listeners.

8

THE EASIEST WAY TO PERSUADE

Get fired up about your subject.

The eloquence brought on by your enthusiasm attracts attention, arouses interest, and triggers action.

Let's assume you were asked to make a speech for the local youth club. You thought the club did good work. You agreed to make the speech. But before the talk you visited the club, talked to executives, to the girls and boys, the counsellors, watched some of the activities, refereed a part of a basketball game. At home you made notes of your impressions of what the club did for youth. You shaped what you had learned into a speech. You gave the speech with the objective of getting your service club to buy twenty memberships to give to needy kids. You got checks for thirty-eight memberships. One of your friends commented, "Chuck, I didn't know you could be so eloquent."

You thought, "Me, eloquent? All I did was tell what the Club did and how I felt its activities benefited those youngsters."

THIS PLAN CAN MAKE ANY SPEAKER ELOQUENT

Note the formula followed by the youth club appeal:

First, get the facts,

Second, decide how you feel about the facts, for or against,

Third, let yourself go–mix facts with your feelings as you recite your story.

A sales manager might put that–

"Sell yourself on what you are selling and it will be easier to sell others on it."

It's a formula that will make any speaker a persuader.

YOUR EMOTIONS AND WORDS AROUSE HIS EMOTIONS

In my speech session I use a chart that reads–

The Tools of Eloquence

- Your Feelings
- His Feelings
- Words

I show the chart and ask, "Which tool is more important in an eloquent appeal?" The discussion on the chart clarifies what we mean by eloquence.

To be most eloquent–

You need to show your emotion,

It helps if your plea is one that the listener can get emotional about, and

Words add to the effect–strong feelings help you think of guttier words.

EMOTION ADDS POWER TO THE FACTS

Facts alone may persuade, but facts plus feelings have greater pulling power. The facts in the youth club speech were there–the club has facilities to handle fifty more. The club can't find fifty with the twenty dollars needed for the camp fee. The speaker suggests that each man in his service club buy one membership and give it to a deserving boy or girl. The club will select the recipients. All facts so far, and enough to form the outline of an interesting speech. But when the speaker told how the work being done affected his feelings, his facts took on life. He told how much he wanted to help, and the listeners asked, "How can we help?" Then he offered his plan. Until he revealed his feelings, he was making an ordinary speech. When his fire started to show, some of the enthusiasm rubbed off on his listeners. Now he explained his plan, so easy, so simple. The friend called him eloquent. Most speakers could be more eloquent if they forgot themselves, their fears of going too far, their possible embarrassment and held back nothing that helped show their feelings and concerns. Getting the money for those memberships became the most important objective in the world to that speaker at that time and the speaker showed it.

WORDS ADD THEIR PART

Speakers tell me, "I don't have the vocabulary for eloquence." I answer, "Forget words. Get steamed up enough and the right words will flow." Where are the impressive words in, "You shall not crucify mankind on a cross of gold?" The feeling behind those words swayed a national political convention. Think of the simple words in, "The only thing we have to fear is fear itself." These words anyone might use sustained an entire nation. You have enough words. Find your cause, assemble the facts, and as you relate those facts, let your feelings show. Listeners want to know if this is how you feel. Too many speakers indicate that this speech is a job the boss sent them to do. Your apparent emotion will cause the listener to ask, "If this speaker's so concerned, maybe I should be too."

YOU CAN HAVE A SILVER TONGUE

One of my speech group protested, "I can't be eloquent. I wasn't born with a silver tongue."

I asked, "Do you ever pray?"

"Yes, every day," he admitted.

"You must have some thought on prayer then," I went on. "I suggest you work up a short speech on prayer, tell your reasons for praying, why you pray, what prayers you use, how you think it helps you."

"The group won't be interested in that," he said.

"Try them and see," I advised. "Make your testimony as strong as you can. Don't hold anything back."

The young man worked up the talk and made it. It was a classic. He talked about thoughts that he had never mentioned to anyone, even to his family or his friends. Here are a few of his ideas—

He started with a story about one of the boys in shipping who had won a prize in the sweepstakes. When he congratulated the winner, the man said, "Someone up there must like me." Then the speaker said, "I believe that someone up there likes me. He hasn't helped me win a sweepstakes yet, but He has helped me. I'll tell you something else—I have great faith in Him, I like Him, I ask His advice, and His help every day. I can cite hundreds of times that He has come through for me."

Other thoughts he expressed were—

He considered prayer as a conversation direct with God.

He talked to God as he might to the man at the next desk.

He forgot words like thee and thou and deign and beseech. God knew such words were not the speaker's words.

He thanked God many times during the day because he believed none of us thanked God enough.

He told how he used prayer to time his isometric exercises.

He finished by asking the group to repeat this prayer with him, "Dear God, I thank *You* for what you have done for me, for faith, family and friends."

ONE SECRET—LET YOUR EMBARRASSMENT SHOW

This speaker knew that many of his listeners might not agree with him. Some might think him some kind of a nut. Others might not go along with the way he prayed, his use of prayer, the words he used, or his belief that prayer helped, but he forgot these thoughts and went all out. It may have been difficult for him to put such thoughts into words before an audience. But at the finish the listeners gave him a standing ovation. I am sure that his presentation persuaded some of his listeners to think a bit more about prayer.

LISTENERS' FEELINGS HELP

A subject like prayer is good because listeners have feelings about it, some for, a few against, some indifferent. This speaker made an eloquent plea for prayer, another who didn't believe in prayer could perhaps make an eloquent speech against it. Either couldn't allow the fear of embarrassment to stop him. He'd have to come clean with his innermost thoughts and feelings.

HOW THE ELOQUENT HANDLE SUBJECTS FOR OR AGAINST

Here is a list of possible general subjects for talks with hints of how you might talk with eloquence either for or against. The wording suggests how to show your strong feelings.

AN IDEA

You say it is sensational–explain why you feel that way. You say, "It stinks"–back that up with facts. "It smells" is good, "It's putrid" may be better. Make a list of the benefits if you are for the idea. Count the negatives if you are against. Talk tough language. You show emotion when you use strong terms. You don't need vulgarities or swear words. There are enough rough words in this language of ours to help cut down any group or idea.

A PLAN

One man tells you, "It's just a lot of money down the drain. These bureaucrats seem to hunt for new drains for our tax money. Another says, "Think of these benefits–" "Which comes first with you–dollars or human needs?"

A CAUSE

One says, "It's against everything we know about people. It can't possibly work. We got enough freeloaders now. You and I working to support them." Another says, "We owe it to these people to give them a chance. The conditions under which they live are not their fault."

A PROJECT

One speaker against the plan hits at the bureaucracy it will set up, "First thing they'll do is hire a director, a political hack, then an assistant director, another hack, and two secretaries. Then these two geniuses hold a meeting and decide they've committed all their budget to salaries. That means they have to ask for more of our money. And they'll get it, because you and I won't get a chance to protest." Another gives ten reasons why this project will be helpful and presents figures to back up what he says. A stranger from another planet wouldn't know the two speakers were talking about the same project.

TV CAN SHOW HOW TO SHAPE YOUR APPEAL

Many of the public interest commercials on TV offer examples of how to persuade. Recall the ones for the Volunteer organization. They tell of the needs of the less fortunate in your town or neighborhood that you might help, then they said, "We want only what you can give. We Want YOU." That "We want you" is the theme of most solicitations–your money, perhaps, or a bit of work, but it is "you" that is wanted. The plea reminds us of how little we are doing for our fellow men. It suggests things we might do without. It tempts us to call the number and ask how we might help. Next time you hear a program that causes you to want to do something, check the appeal the solicitor used. These same appeals will help you be eloquent when you speak about your causes.

FACTS ALONE NEED HELP

Too many speakers think that the logic of their facts will enlist followers. With a small percentage of listeners facts may be enough. But it is easier to attract all if you arouse their emotions. The plan you are against will take some rights from them. You know that nobody wants to lose any rights. You mention this loss in a way that makes listeners say, "They can't do this to us." Then you add, "That's exactly what these crooks are preparing to do."

HOW TO STRENGTHEN FACTS WITH EMOTION

The eloquent combine facts and emotion and words. They damn the project of the other side with words such as, "The million dollars was to build homes for one hundred families. Now the million dollars are spent and how many homes are ready for occupancy–a measly three homes. That's right–three houses. Three lousy fifteen thousand dollar homes for a million bucks. That's the kind of bargains bureaucracy gives you. Now the Authority has the nerve to ask for another million dollars to produce more bargains. Maybe this time they will produce four homes

TOUGH TALK HELPS

You may say, "That's tough talk."

But you have to agree that tough talk shows how you feel. It also has more power to sway opinion. This type of talk is illustrated all through the examples that follow. Think of these–down the drain–free loaders–director and assistant director–all of the budget for payroll–all bring negative thoughts to the listener, all show him how he should feel.

THE FIRE OF ELOQUENCE STARTS CONFLAGRATIONS

A teacher of speaking must describe eloquence as a persuasive device. If you feel strongly enough about anything to speak with feeling about it, you can persuade others to look more favorably on that anything.

First, sell yourself why your anything will help your listener, and,

Second, go all out in telling your listener why it will help. Your conviction plus your display of emotion will give you the eloquence you need.

Don't look for eloquence when a speaker starts: I am not too sure about this–

He might have a great cause and a most complete vocabulary, but he is not about to sway you with his oratory.

But when he starts: "Have I got something to tell you today!" the chances favor your hearing a speech with facts and feeling.

THE RIGHT SUBJECT HELPS YOU BE EMOTIONAL

All through this chapter I have stressed the fact that your subject should excite you. When you have strong feelings about your subject you'll find it easier to be eloquent. Your sympathy, your compassion, your desire to help will show through on a subject you are for. If you're against, your hostility, your contempt, your outrage will be apparent. No matter what side you are on, don't try to repress your feelings, let them hang out as you let yourself go.

SIX WAYS ELOQUENCE PERSUADES

These facts about listeners can help you shape any eloquence that attempts to persuade:

1. They want to help in deserving causes. They want to be counted among the good. Think of the mothers who go out on Mothers March. Tell your listeners how they can enlist.
2. They are willing to do their part. Bring them news of what they can do, describe it as easy and simple.
3. The don't want to stand idly by watching others do work on which they should be helping. Let them know all are welcome. Some may be afraid of a rebuff if they volunteer.
4. Suggest the next best help. If they can't do what you ask, they wonder how they can help.
5. Listeners welcome any idea that shows them how they can get more satisfaction out of life. Show them how they can get into the swing.
6. All are complimented by your assumption that they are the kind of people who will give or work for a good cause.

Shape your talk to tell them these facts. Perhaps not all of them apply to your appeal, but bear heavily on the ones that do.

9

YOUR FEELINGS MAKE YOU ELOQUENT

Rev up your feelings and you become eloquent:

For your cause.

For God and country.

Against the other's cause.

Against injustice.

Some of the heat you generate will show in your voice, in what you say, and how you say it. One speech instructor puts it, "Get your feelings out on your sleeve where we can see them and we will feel them."

ELOQUENCE CHANGES YOUR IMAGE

Perhaps you have attended a session of a class in public speaking where the instructor assigns another student to hit you with a rolled newspaper while you speak. With another furnishing the action you sound off with emotion. You're disgusted because you allowed yourself to be put in this embarrassing position, you hate the joker who is enjoying pummeling you, you despise the instructor who put you on this spot. And those feelings take over. You speak as you've never spoken before. The good guys become saints, the bad guys ravening wolves in sheep's clothing.

What you say comes over with force and gusto. You forget that you are the third assistant computer programmer. You're a tiger. What you say and how you say it shows the listeners a different you. Now you are a knight in shining armor seeking justice for the oppressed or a Florence Nightingale shedding tears as she asks help for the sick and afflicted. The pounding with the rolled newspaper is one way speech instructors build a fire under, or stick a pin in, speakers. The instructor developed that stunt to get you to forget yourself and sound off uninhibitedly.

LET YOUR FEELINGS SHOW

You'll hear no eloquence from the fellow who feels it is safer to sit on the fence watching the world go by. The eloquent take sides, they are part of it, they help the good or fight the evil. The eloquent don't slouch or lean on a lectern. They stand on the balls of their feet, flex their muscles, put up their dukes, and come out fighting. Let's say you tell a friend about an idea. He listens but offers no comment. You don't know whether he is for or against it, do you? It's different when he says, "That's a screwy idea." You know where he stands. And suppose he says, "That's a great idea?" He's a Daniel come to judgment, isn't he? Most listeners approve the speaker who has an opinion and states it with vigor for or against.

ASK TO BE DEALT A HAND

That's what the eloquent do. They give. Their words are colored by emotion. Somewhere I read, "Emotion is the foundation of eloquence." One popular speaker says, "Have enough feeling for your cause, the words will come to you." The speaker on the soap box on the corner shouts, "Wait till I get off this damn collar and tie and I'll give it to you straight." The feeling he puts into tearing off that collar and tie shows how much he hates a society that puts men in collars and ties.

Listeners would rate him as a good speaker, crazy ideas, perhaps, but all would agree on his ability as a speaker. And he got that "good" rating because he showed his feelings. Without that revelation he might have had trouble getting people to notice him or to pause long enough to hear more than a few words.

STOKE UP THE FIRE

You have heard speakers talk about a subject of great interest to you. They had strong arguments, but they put no life into their drab, colorless presentations. You wondered, "Why was this dope selected to do this talk?" You felt that without preparation you could do better. On the wall of my office is a headline, clipped from a magazine that says, "If you got something uninteresting to say, get somebody interesting to say it." Any feeling you show in a talk is interesting. Without interest in your subject, you can't expect to be eloquent.

FEELING STAMPS YOU AS A HUMAN BEING

You see the truth of this in TV commercials. The advertiser has hired a big name to tell about his remedy. In some cases the deal paid off. But in too many the big name showed no interest or feeling. The sponsors had hired a beautiful voice and perfect diction, but had not enlisted his feelings. The person who developed that remedy and lived through the testing of it would have done better. The developer of that remedy knew how the victims suffered, knew how the remedy brought relief, quickly and for long periods. Strengthened by such knowledge, feelings would dominate the presentation.

YOUR EMBARRASSMENT HELPS EMPHASIZE

Listeners are swayed when you show it. I complimented a speaker on a plea she had made. She thanked me, then added, "I'm wrapped up in the subject. There were tears in my eyes when I finished." Her speech was for sponsorship of refugee families. Those tears strengthened her appeal. No listener could doubt her testimony. You see the power of feeling in the newer popular singers on TV. They seem to hurt all over as they mouth the simple words "I love you, baby." You wonder why they display the tears, the wails and the pain until the song is ended and you hear the tremendous applause. A friend says, "The more it hurts, the more applause. No tune, no voice, no words, no melody, just the plaintive cry and evidence of excruciating pain."

You may feel embarrassed when you expose your intimate thoughts to your audience. But that embarrassment helps. The listeners sense it, they too feel embarrassed for you, and they admire you for being brave enough to show your intimate feelings. Forget any embarrassment you feel. Talk about your ambitions, your dreams, your fears. What is wrong if your words show your innermost feelings? That's how you feel, that's where you stand and your sincerity registers. If it helps in winning recruits, workers or contributions, let your feelings show.

TIPS ON SHOWING YOUR FEELINGS

Here are some thoughts on putting feeling into what you say.

1. *Charge Your Batteries:* Remember how you feel on those cold winter mornings when you try to start your car and you get only a reluctant grind from the starter. You feel mighty low, don't you? Listeners have that same kind of reaction from the speaker who seems to have trouble starting. It is not enough to say, "I'm enthusiastic," or, "I'm concerned." Show how you feel. Show you are angry, madder than a wet hen. Show you are glad, enthusiastic, overjoyed. Put your feelings out for all to see. That's what eloquent speaking is all about.

2. *Rehearse Your Feelings:* At a sales meeting I heard a trainer drill his sales people, both men and women, in saying these words—"I'm enthusiastic about this benefit."

He asked each one in turn to stand and repeat the words a number of times. The first efforts were not too good, the second better, the third better still. When he felt the sales people showed the right amount of conviction, he said, "Now, describe this benefit with that much enthusiasm."

With that bit of rehearsal each salesman's voice showed that he was convinced the customer was lucky to get the benefit.

The drill had built a fire under the salesmen. When you have a speaking assignment, keep telling yourself about the pluses you have to present. A recording can say, "I'm enthusiastic about this idea." You can read the words from a written script and not convey your feelings adequately. Condition yourself mentally and the listener will see you are enthusiastic. You can't listen to an enthusiastic speaker without some enthusiasm rubbing off on you.

3. *Use the Confession:* I told of the talk on prayer. It would be difficult to disguise your feelings in a description of why you pray and how you pray. To explain your prayer thoughts and habits you have to bring up thoughts and feelings that are seldom discussed. And as some of the group agree with you, they think of similar reactions they have. Opening your heart is good for showing compassion for the underdog, the unfortunate, the stricken. You feel sorry, you wonder how you can help, you have so much, they have so little. But you don't help by being sorry unless you do something. And so this is what you did. Of course you had doubts, you feared you didn't have the skill, you feared you would be rejected. You feared this, and that. But you tried and your help was much more welcome than you dreamed.

By sharing your reactions you move closer to your listeners. You develop an intimacy that helps make you one of them.

4. *Stress the Achievement Theme:* The Horatio Alger idea can sway others. This week I read of the undersize boy who wanted to be a basketball player, but the larger boys wouldn't let him play. He struggled against his size, practiced in all his spare time, and years later became a top player in the N.B.A. I cut out the story and gave it to a small boy in the neighborhood who has that handicap of size. Remember stories about the one who struggles to lift himself out of the slums or who has to work hard for his education or who overcomes a physical handicap. Such stories have the power to lift you out of yourself to sway listeners. Listeners agree that if we do nothing we slip further into our rut, that if we do something we have a chance to lift

ourselves to the heights. Psychologists agree that most of us use only a fraction of our ability. Most are content to go along as we are. A story of what others have done can cause us to wonder why we don't do something to change our status.

5. *Use the "We Need You" Appeal:* You see this used in the "Volunteer" campaign mentioned in Chapter 8. We all want to be needed. The Big Brothers use this appeal and thousands are recruited to help as substitute fathers of boys that have no fathers in their homes. The other day a retired head of a manufacturing firm told me, "I was going crazy in retirement until I found that there are so many people who need some kind of help." He was calling on shut-ins, taking some to doctors, making purchases for others. "I get a great kick out of it," he said. "When I was working I stayed so close to that grindstone that I didn't know how much help of this kind was needed." Realize that most listeners want to do something for their fellow man. They hesitate to make the first move. They need urging. Speak of an activity with emotion and some of these holdbacks will enlist.

6. *Bring in "How You Gain" Testimony:* The listeners know they are to be asked to give when they come to the meeting. They start figuring how little or if they can duck giving entirely. They think of their bucks as going down the drain along with contributions to other such charities. They see themselves losing money. But when you list what they gain—pride in being a giver—thrill when hearing the new organ—membership with a group of concerned citizens. Tell them of their gain and your project looks different to them. The head of a great New York banking house told a group soliciting memberships for a cause, "Every time I attend one of these meetings I see so many of the same faces. I call them the 'Good Guys.' They are that, because they are the ones who carry the burden of keeping so many helpful activities going." I am sure my chest expanded a bit as I heard those words. Here I was a member of this elite group—the ones who get involved. List how the listener gains and your story will have greater appeal.

LISTENERS ADMIRE THE ELOQUENT

Eloquence is not all big mouth, not all words, phrases, slogans. The poet says, "I speak with my heart." The speaker needs that same formula. Another poet says–

> I have to say the things I feel
> I have to feel the things I say.

You can do both, I know. Prove it to yourself by trying to make an eloquent statement. Select a subject about which you have strong feelings for or against, a subject such as–

the environment

the taxes we pay and politicians waste

today's permissiveness.

Collect data on the subject. Talk to friends about it. In your next speech tear into it. Let your hair fall into disorder. Let your feelings show. You'll be surprised at how eloquent you can be.

10

WANTS AND DESIRES HELP YOU BE ELOQUENT

"The line between eloquence and horsefeathers is mighty thin." A successful speaker is responsible for that statement.

The one who agrees with the appeal might call the speech eloquence.

The one who disagrees might call it horsefeathers.

Tell listeners that they are intelligent, good citizens, that they have more friends than they imagine, and what you say is eloquent to them. Say the opposite and they question your judgment. Partisans think that anything favorable you say about their cause is eloquent. They embrace you because you are a brother, a highly intelligent brother. Say anything against their cause and they stop listening. The poet has put it, "We want to listen to what we want to hear." The speaker becomes more eloquent when listeners hear what they want to hear.

ELOQUENCE COMES EASIER IF YOU USE WHAT YOU KNOW ABOUT PEOPLE

Use what you know about listeners' wants and needs when you speak to others. They want–

1. to belong
2. to feel that they are accomplishing something worthwhile.
3. recognition–a build-up of their self-esteem
4. acceptance by their friends and associates
5. security for themselves and families
6. freedom to use their own heads, do jobs their way.

Appeals to these six wants sound eloquent to listeners. Here are some ideas on how to use what you know about all of us.

1. SHOW THEY BELONG AND THEY ARE INCLINED TO GO ALONG

In any group there are some that most speakers seem to leave out. Usually these are the little people, the ones who have the strongest desire to be included. The speaker's plea is to the brass, as if the lower-rated do not count. One of my speaker friends says, "Include them in." The "in" doesn't seem necessary, but it emphasizes the yearning of the little people. The line, "Our kind of people," has pull when it includes the high and low. It says that we are equal, together, family. "Team up with your buddies" is an appeal that includes the ones that feel left out.

2. THEY LIKE ANY CHALLENGE

Listeners want to produce. They go for talk that mentions their ability to do better. A sales manager asks one salesman to make 27 calls per day instead of the 15 that the sales force thought a reasonable quota. He takes the salesperson aside and says, "Let's try an experiment that will show these others how those extra calls will increase sales. Don't tell anybody you are doing it, just do it." You may ask, "Is that eloquence?" It is a challenge to the person's ability. The one challenged would like to see what can be accomplished. The same appeal can be used to get new members for the club. "Last year we got four in July, this year let's set a quota of ten." You get eloquent when you use lines like–

"Let's show where we stand."

"Why shouldn't you get involved?"

"This cry for help is one with which listeners will agree."

Success Stories Help Recruit: To accomplish anything, listeners have to want to enough. They may have to brush aside obstacles or drive through them. The speaker approaches eloquence by using the story of Sarah or Joe, the handicapped youngster with–

no money

no education

no experience

no powerful friends

But listen to what Sarah or Joe did. Then the eloquent adds, "If it could be accomplished with all those obstacles, think of what you can do."

3. COMPLIMENTS WIN FOLLOWERS

There is an old saying, "There is no more pleasing gift than a compliment." You have been asked to take jobs in civic activities and you were quick with such protests as–

I have no time

I've got a new load of work

I am not good at that sort of thing

I don't like that kind of work

But your defense crumbled when the one with the request adds–

we need somebody with your standing, your skills, your efficiency

someone the members will respect
someone we can count on to get the job done

Note how these appeals tie in with the desires of all of us—

we want the respect of others
we want to help out in good causes
we want others to tell us we are important

Tilling the Soil of Vanity Pays: To some degree we are all vain. We like to be praised, patted on the back, included with the right-thinking people. To use a remark that compliments us is eloquence, even one that stretches the facts a bit. The speaker says, "Intelligent adults like you." Some may smile at such a designation, but the smile accompanies the thought that the speaker is rather discerning, has perception, knows quality when he sees it. Try the line some time and note the effect.

There's a Big Appeal in "You Can Do Anything"

Most listeners have some doubt. They need strong urging to get them to try. Youth leaders report that it is difficult to get promising youngsters to think of themselves as leaders. They pass up the committee jobs that would give them training for the higher posts. The leaders use appeals like—

"The experience will be valuable"
"Get the knack of doing this and you can go far"
"Think of the satisfaction you'll get out of the job well done"

Ask the listener to do better and your challenge brings up the question, "Why shouldn't I?" Often they are doing well now but so often they have vowed to do better. You know everybody wants to accomplish more; thus you are together in the appeal.

Forget the Skeptics: Laugh at those who say that praise, applause, flattery or compliments are largely the old oil. Admit it is. But it wins friends. Isn't that where the term "oil" originated—a little more grease for the wheels? When you want others to do something for your cause, you need friends. Tell your committee, "The club selected us, because members respect every one of us." Who will argue about that? Not one of the committee. Build your compliments on honesty and truth. It is not too difficult.

4. SCORE BY STRESSING THEIR ACCEPTANCE

"You're one of us."

"Without workers like you this club wouldn't be what it is today."

Many listeners feel like outsiders, even though for years they have been members in good standing of the group. They think of the management of the club or business as "They," not "We." One manager put it, "There are too many loners in my group; they don't feel they are part of the department." In a speech the plan you offer was devised by "They"; it is for the benefit of "Them." Your audience for your speech may be packed into a small room. The individuals might reach out and touch perhaps four or five others. But they have no assurance that these others accept them as members of the group. They ask, "Why should I make calls or contribute or give time?" The eloquent answer that question by stating that the listeners are the kind of people that want to help their fellow men. Baloney, you say. Agree again, but you know it is the kind of baloney that results in activity.

Note How Business Does It: To promote more togetherness, companies run social and sports programs to give the employee a feeling of acceptance. When the employees join a bowling team, they play with a group that shows they accept him by the rooting they do for him. Good or bad as a bowler, they pull for the member of their team. And these bowling buddies get to know each other and think better of each other. The acceptance as one of us is apparent. Club groups send out inquiries asking the new member what committee he would like to serve on. They know that appointment to a committee shows that the new member is accepted. Any work that he is asked to do on a committee emphasizes the fact that he is wanted, needed.

Use These Acceptance Terms: The speaker uses this appeal when referring to listeners as–we–us–our plan–our results. Such terms indicate that every one of the listeners had a part in the success or can have it. You've heard athletes explain the success of their team with remarks like–"We got a wonderful bunch of people, all friends, all working together, no prima donnas. All season when somebody slumped, another player came on to hold us up. You can't beat that kind of team." The eloquent will emphasize this point with words like–team–family–group–clan–crew–gang–unit–department. They will speak of harmony–rapport–unity–team work–cooperation–coordination. Eloquence doesn't play up Captains and Kings. It goes overboard on the small people working shoulder to shoulder, on a "one-for-all-all-for-one" basis. And this kind of talk moves listeners because they want to be accepted.

5. PLAY UP THE PROMISE OF SECURITY

You may ask, "How can a promise of security be eloquent?" You hear it constantly on the TV commercials. Think of the remedies that fight pain, colds, bad breath, body odors, dandruff, falling hair, hair that won't stay in place, dry skin, oily skin, dishpan hands. If you think security has little appeal, why did you buy the different kinds of insurance you are paying for–life, health, hospital, fire, liability? Because you feel you and your family need protection. Right? You want to feel secure. Employers use the same appeal with pensions, 25-year clubs, hospitalization, unemployment insurance, stock plans, profit sharing. Environmental groups are working to clean up our air and water. It seems that all around us others are working to help us feel secure. The speaker who talks about helping make our future more secure can be eloquent to us.

Assurance Moves Listeners: I tell you that you can make a good speech. You like that thought but you say, "Even the thought of standing before a group makes me ill." I recite a list of benefits to you. You ask yourself, "What am I? Man or mouse?" Then I use the assurance question, "What have you got to lose?" You know the answer to that–nothing. Listen to a group sing–

"We will overcome"
or
"Happy days are here again"
or
"When the roll is called up yonder."

The singers' emotion indicates what they want when they sing these lines. The writers of those lyrics knew what people wanted. All such songs appeal to the listener's desire for security.

WIN FRIENDS BY OFFERING WHAT LISTENERS WANT

The listener's wants and desires help you be eloquent. You know how they feel on many subjects. Use what you know about their wants and desires and you will seem much more eloquent to them.

11

FACILITY WITH WORDS SHAPES YOUR ELOQUENCE

A large vocabulary does not make you eloquent. You may call your opponent–

"A dirty crook." With a bit more thought you could make that–

"A despicable crook."

Couldn't you put more feeling into that second tag?

The feeling you put into your words is not helped by a large vocabulary.

YOU USE ALL OF THE WORDS IN THESE LINES–

"Never in the field of human conflict has so much been owed by so many to so few."

"Give me liberty or give me death."

"I only regret that I have but one life to give for my country."

"Yesterday, December 7, 1941—a date which will live in infamy—"

In a time of stress the speakers of these lines all used simple words, words you might use every day. Yet historians rate the words as eloquent. The speakers said something, they showed strong feelings, and the simple words plus the feeling they put into them made for eloquence.

FIVE WAYS THAT WORDS CAN HELP YOU BE ELOQUENT

1. In word selection, one word is better than another.
2. With three-word combinations.
3. With three-phrase combinations.
4. With words of opposite meaning.
5. Watch euphemisms.

Let's review how easy it is:

1. THE STRONGER WORD HELPS

Some words are stronger than others. Some present a better picture. There are words that convey strength, others that indicate weakness. Think of the picture that these words convey—

Godliness
cleanliness
honesty

As you look at them, you think of other words that convey a similar idea of "good."

Then think of the meaning of—

Sinful
weak
crooked
disgraceful.

Again add words that convey a similar meaning. Now think of additions to these words of joy—

glory
hosanna

hallelujah
hurrah
happy days.

Do the same with these words of trouble—

adversity
hardship
poverty
frustration.

and the words of promise

plans
objectives
goals
destiny.

Then think of the names for persons that are belittling

nobody
small cog
pipsqueak

and the opposites such as

leader
driving force

These exercises show that you know enough words.

A Similar List of Words for the Enemy's Appeal May Help

You don't like the plan, the arguments for it, or the appeal. A list like this helps—horsefeathers—blue-sky—eyewash—bushwa—guff—piffle—nuts—assininity—pipe dream—whimsy—delirium—apparition—dream—hallucination—brainstorm—meaningless—confusing—bewildering—hysteria—chimera—aberration—foolishness—naivete—fantasy—imbecility—paranoia—nonsense—absurdity—stupidity—inexperience—gullibility—ghastly.

Describe the enemy and his plan in stronger words and listeners can measure how high your feelings run.

Make a List of Names for the Enemy

There are scores of words that can show your praise or contempt. This list should give you an idea–fat heads–nitwits–wretches–bird brains–holes in their heads–eggheads–fools–hypocrites–windbags–hot air artists–blackguards–liars–deadbeats – cheapskates – low lifes – no goods – zeros – rabble–fossils – bleeding-hearts – do-gooders – political hacks– scalawags – crooks – criminals – charlatans – horse-thieves – swindlers–unscrupulous – unprincipled – loafers – scoundrels – thieves – highwaymen. As you glance through the list, you may think of other names, stronger, and more in keeping with how you feel about the enemy. When I read this list in a speaking class, one young woman said, "I'd never use some of those words." "But you'd use some of them?" I asked. She named a few, the word "crook" was one of them. "Ok, when you say crook, let your voice emphasize the fact that you think they are 'dirty crooks' or 'despicable crooks.' "

There Is a Variety for GOOD

File some of these for use–righteous–upright–virtuous–honest –true–just–benevolent–moral–honorable–conscientous–reputable–strong–healthy.

Then the Offer

It offers–something we have always wanted–benefits –advantages–profits–convenience–boon–gain–blessings–opportunity–better health–freedom–prosperity–milk and honey–achievement–consummation–victory–enjoyment–peace and plenty. The list you make up should include all good words that might apply. Some to one cause, others to another. But when you use the good words, include only those you can say with a straight face. This caution is more important on your favorable words. Go overboard on the negatives you apply to the enemy, his cause and his arguments, but don't exaggerate on the positives that apply to your side. You might sound like the announcers on TV who claim too much.

2. SERIES OF THREE WORDS ADD EMPHASIS

Speakers add strength to their speech by using words in

strings of three. The words have about the same meaning and they give the force of repetition. Here are some three-word combinations I have culled from speeches:

greedy, grasping, avaricious
cheap, stingy, niggardly
eager, pushing, selfish
gourmet, glutton, pig
alive, alert, eager
meaningless, confusing, bewildering
rude, egotistical, contemptuous
dictatorial, despotic, overbearing.

As you study these combinations you think of words that might strengthen the thought expressed. Each combination of three words can be spoken with a rhythm that is easy on the ears. Can't you imagine a speaker putting feeling into—

"It's meaningless, confusing, yes, even bewildering."

Let the Meaning Build Up

In working up the three-word combos, think of the "good, better, best" idea. Place the strongest word last. Examine again this one—

dictatorial, despotic, overbearing

Do you feel that "overbearing" is the strongest word? If not, you can speak the line with more force by changing the order so that the word you think strongest comes last. "Overbearing" is a rather soft word. Perhaps you can speak the line better as—

overbearing, despotic, dictatorial.

As you say the line, put your feeling against dictators into that last word.

Add the Third Word in These Examples

Check your skill on these examples—

massive, decisive, and (what?)
meaningful, realistic and (what?)
agility, ability and (what?)
mighty, noble and (what?)

You filled in the gaps and the third word was not too difficult to find. Yes, you can use this device. Right?

How to Make Three-Word Combinations More Eloquent

Here are some thoughts to help with your three-word combinations:

Select Your Three Words: Find three that have the same or similar meanings. If you wanted to depreciate your competitor's idea you might come up with this list–theory–assumption–speculation – conjecture – dream – fantasy – imagination. What three would you select?

Arrange the Words to Build Up or Tear Down: The three words should have a logical buildup, a logical tear down or a logical hysteria. The "Good, better, best" mentioned illustrates the buildup. "Sidelined, crippled, decimated" demonstrates the tear down. "Ambiguous, illusory, incredible" may represent the hysteria.

Select Words That Speak Best: The final word of the three helps more if it is one you can speak with force. That third word gives the snap of the whip. Think of this three–"Greedy, grasping, avaricious." You can say that last word with snap, can't you? How about–cheap, stingy, niggardly–eager, pushing, selfish–gourmet, glutton, pig? All allow you to put feeling into that third word. If you feel that you can put more contempt into the second or first word of your three, put the favored word at the end. Always practice saying the three words. Try to explode on that last word.

Use Three Words Instead of Four: This tip applies to words, phrases, sentences. The addition of one or two words usually spoils the rhythm of the speaking. Try saying this three–

"He's biased, bigoted, stupid."

The three words roll out gracefully, don't they;

Now try saying aloud–

"He's biased, bigoted, ignorant, stupid."

You lost steam somewhere, didn't you?

Now try saying aloud these that I have heard speakers use–

"It brings on anger, distemper, depression, frayed nerves."

"The boy was tubbed, scrubbed, manicured, deodorized."

Cut the manicured from that last line and try it again. It went better, didn't it. –tubbed, scrubbed and deodorized. You might like it better as, tubbed, scrubbed and manicured.

You have heard the Churchhill line, "I have nothing to offer but blood, toil, tears and sweat."

Note four words–blood, toil, tears, sweat. Try speaking that line aloud with the four words. Then leave out one of the words and speak it with three. You do better with three, don't you? Perhaps that's why so often when you see this line quoted one of the words is left out.

3. THREE PHRASES ADD RHYTHM

This is another device that speakers use for emphasis and repetition. Note this example–

> "Our rivers are so cruddy that–
> fish can't live in them *(pause)*
> people can't drink from them, *(pause)*
> and *(pause)*
> kids can't swim in them."

Try saying the first two of those phrases without the third. You lose some of the force, don't you?

Here are other examples–

> "To cultivate wisdom we have–
> to recognize it *(pause)*
> to study it, and *(pause)*
> to put what we learn to use."

> "When we consider our record, you can say–
> that much has been done, *(pause)*
> that much can be measured, and *(pause)*
> that much remains to be done."

This pause gives emphasis to the second and third ideas. Note that in the first phrases "to" has been used with each phrase. In the second, "That" has been used with each. In writing for reading, "that" and "to" would have been used once with the first line. But the phrases speak better if you say the words with each phrase.

Simple Wording Goes Over Better: The ideas in these phrases are stated in simple words. When you ask a listener to follow three thoughts, don't complicate his problem with words that can mean one thing to you and another to him. Put your thought in simple words and he has a better chance of understanding.

4. WORDS OF OPPOSITE MEANINGS HEIGHTEN THE EFFECT

Another form of the apt use of words is the combination of opposites for example–from rags to riches. This device is used with single words and/or phrases. For instance here are some I have heard–

Single words–

rain to sunshine
gloom to joy
interest instead of boredom
depression to euphoria
do rather than doubt
lead rather than influence
not doubting but believing

Phrases–

making good instead of making excuses
looking for faults instead of looking for advantages
bringing up doubts instead of hopes
working for change instead of the status quo.

5. WATCH EUPHEMISMS

The nice way of saying a thing is easy on the feelings but most euphemisms can't add force to what you say. Try saying aloud–

"He passed away"
You can't put much feeling into those words, can you?

Now say aloud–

"He worked himself to death for us."

You do better on that, and your listener gets a picture of the martyr struggling on against odds, until his poor body could take no more. The nice way of saying things can't convey the strength, belief, or compassion you may want. Think of Whittier's line–

Who touches a hair of yon grey head
Dies like a dog!–

He didn't say "will be shot" or "will be courtmartialed." No, he pictured him dying in the gutter, with his comrades marching off, afraid to look in his direction.

WORDS PLUS FEELING REGISTER ELOQUENTLY

You can be eloquent with the words you know now. Let's say you want to call the enemy–

a nobody

a wash out

a false prophet

You know those words, right?

Put your feeling of disparagement into the way you say the words and you become eloquent. Think of the kind of nobody he is, lower than low, isn't he? Despicable? Dishonest? Given to delusions of grandeur? Show you feel he is not just a harmless nobody. He is a dangerous enemy. Beware! Think this way about the feeling you put into your words and you can be as eloquent as anybody.

TIPS ON HANDLING YOUR WORDS

Collecting material is closely connected with words. The idea you collect is in words. Better speakers know how to get the most out of those words through substitution, arranging and handling. Here are some thoughts on composition:

1. *Cut the Number of Words:* You hear others say, "At this point in time." What's wrong with "Now." The speaker who says, "To make a long story short–" has the right idea, but

hasn't he added a number of words with that which doesn't further his story.

2. *Rule Out Fancy Words:* Check out such words as "redundant," "sanguine" or, "unilateral." Good words all, and you may know what they mean. But how many of your listeners will? One speaker friend says that he checks out every word with seven or more letters. Most of these fancy words have substitutes that everybody can define.

3. *Say It Direct:* It may sound classy to say, "Like the Romans of old, we can't–" Keep the Romans out of it, and tell what we can't do. Explain what we can do, clearly. Too many listeners are sent home without ever hearing what the speaker wanted them to do.

4. *Use "You," "Yours," Often:* Don't allow listeners to forget that they are the ones to do this job, or carry this banner. Instead of speaking of people in general, make your proposal a personal one for those in the room. Stress, "This means you."

5. *Adopt a Conversational Tone:* Use contractions if you do in ordinary speech with friends. "We are opposed" breaks speech rhythm. You sound more natural saying, "We're opposed." Forget "We cannot–" Say, "We can't."

6. *Check Out Roundabout Expressions:* "Scram," speaks better than "Make yourself scarce." And it gets faster action. The Commander didn't say, "Please be advised to retain control of the vessel until further notice." He ordered, "Don't give up the ship."

7. *Use Words That Promise:* Use words that mechanically describe your idea and add words that promise something for the listeners; words like–benefit–assistance–advantage–convenience–ease–profit–gain–addition–saving.

8. *Avoid Trite Expressions:* In introducing you, the toastmaster might have used, "Without further ado I give you–"Take no cue from him. Forget such as, "In my brief experience–," "I know I am taking an unpopular stand–" What you say tells the listener these things.

9. *Use Short Sentences:* Use as few words as possible. Say, "Our best man has the flu." No need to add how he got it or

anything of the kind. You have explained why he is not playing. Adding clauses and asides can make your point more difficult to understand.

10. *Short Paragraphs Give Relief:* Break your remarks up into short paragraphs. After each paragraph you'll pause, and allow what you say to sink in. The pause gives the listener a relief that he craves.

11. *Forget Demanding Words:* You know how you hate to be ordered around. Cut any authoritative words, any threats. No "we must," or, "we have to," or, "you got to do this," or, "you better go along." Persuasive reasons why are easier to take.

12. *Be Yourself:* Most speeches are stilted. Perhaps it is because of the stage fright that comes from speaking before a group. Don't try to put on. Use the same type of talk that you would use with the person at the next desk.

13. *Use Questions That Include Listeners:* Tell them how it is, but use a question now and then to determine if they believe, agree, or feel the way you do. The question brings them in. They may not have a chance to answer, but their faces tell you if they understand and are with you. What you see on those faces can tell you to change tack, or offer more explanation. Your most useful question may be, "Am I making myself clear?"

14. *Check for Clarity Beforehand:* If you have written a script, ask two or more associates to read it and tell you what it means. If they discover any parts that are not clear, change those statements to make them understandable.

15. *Repeat Only to Clarify or Emphasize:* Most of us before an audience have a tendency to yak on and on. There are times when repetition is useful, but in most situations the one statement will register the idea.

16. *Cut Additions:* The most popular phrase today with the TV salesmen is "and more." They list a number of specifics and then add, "And more." Speakers use, "and so forth and so on," "in any way, shape or form," "if you please." Drop all such extras.

17. *No Depreciation:* If you have only a poor visual, don't

apologize for it. Forget, "I know it's difficult to see these figures." Why should listeners join up with a speaker who can't produce a good visual? If you're not good at reciting poetry, skip any mention of that fact. Recite and listeners will know Skip reciting and it is your secret.

18. *Avoid Groping:* Try to hide any speech habits such as "ums" and "ahs." Think of your objective, not of words you use and the proper words will tumble out. Correct nervous habits, no pulling at your tie, scratching your head, heisting your belt. Such habits take away from your message.

19. *Mistakes in Grammar:* You may say, "They know what I mean, don't they?" They do, but they learn more about you from such mistakes. It is easy to correct the seven mistakes you hear most often.

20. *Watch Your Attitude:* Show by your words and manner that you are happy with this opportunity to speak to this group. Act as if every listener is a customer or a prospective contributor or worker in your cause. Hold them high in your opinion and they will be more inclined to go along with you.

12

HOW TO FIND ELOQUENT MATERIAL

It seems speakers are continually yakking at us—

in meetings
on the radio and TV
on recordings.

Some of the talk stirs us, inspires, persuades. Some of it gets to us.

Ok, why not analyze what the speaker—

says, and how he says it
does, and how he socks it to us
appeals, how he lays it on our laps.
and clearly outlines what he wants from us.

There is no reason why we can't use the same techniques.

If a speaker can use certain devices to get you steamed up, why can't you use the same devices to get others steamed up?

WHERE SPEAKERS GET THEIR MATERIAL

I have studied eloquent speeches in talks and recordings and most of the material used came from—

the speaker's experience

his reading, and

the oratory of others.

Any eloquent material you need can come from these sources. There follows some thoughts on how.

HOW TO SHAPE YOUR EXPERIENCES

In a day lots of things happen to you or around you. Think back to yesterday and you'll probably remember ten or more. "Yeah, but they're not worth mentioning," you say.

Why not? Let's assume that as you stepped into the lobby of your office building a beautiful blonde rushed up to you, threw her arms around you, kissed you and said, "Oh, Harry, I'm so glad to see you." Your name's not Harry, you never saw this woman before—

You're glad your spouse didn't see this.

You know such an incident would be worth mentioning.

Let's assume you are a woman executive on her first management job and have a similar experience. You walk into your office building lobby. A big lug yells, "Babe," and throws his arms around you, knocking your spectacles awry in his enthusiasm. You never were called "Babe" by anybody, you never saw the gorilla before. You're sure that a number of people who report to you saw the incident. But out of the ten experiences you had yesterday, you didn't rate one as being as newsworthy as that.

And so when your spouse asks, "How did your day at the office go? You answer, "So, so."

You say nothing happened.

But how about the shoeshine boy that tried to sell you a football pool ticket as he does every week? And what did you think about the boss ruining the office meeting beefing about the trouble he is having with his expensive car. Bosses are like that and you tuned out on him. But remember what he told the service men and what they told him is the type of stuff that listeners love to hear. Yesterday you didn't see a fire, an accident, or a guy threatening to jump out of a tenth story window. But things did happen. And those things are the kind of material that listeners love to hear.

Look for the Human Interest: Let's say you burned when the shoeshine boy in the office lobby tried to sell you a football pool ticket. No great sin in buying a football ticket, but it is against the law and you know that some racketeer runs that pool. You feel the same gangster may be behind the drug pushers that try to sell dope to the kids at high school.

Do you see any possibilities in that idea? Next the boss calls an office meeting to discuss making better use of time. You think this is a good idea. Then he wastes most of the meeting time beefing about the performance of his ten thousand dollar car.

Do you see possibilities in that theme?

Ideas can be developed from almost any experience. The bus driver growls at you. The garage attendant takes over your car and races up the ramp at what you think is 60 miles per hour. All is grist for the mill.

Everyday Experiences Go Best: This is because similar things happen to your listeners. One great help is your memory of the past. Remember any of your dreams when you were young? Your frustrations when you first entered business, remember any? These will go over big because you lived through them and can't hide your feelings as you tell about them.

Talk about the small farm you lived on, how evenings after the chores were done you sat on the grass out in front and waved to the people going down the road. You'd imagine they were bound for the far-off places, China, Singapore, Malay. You knew they were going down to the supper at the Baptist Church, but you liked to think of those places you read about in your atlas. You told yourself that someday you would visit those places, all of them. At other times you looked down in the valley to the west and you saw the white church steeple that stood out against the green hills in the distance. When the red glow was on the sky at sunset you thought of Aunt Rose's saying, "Red sky at night, a sailor's delight." Through the years every time you have seen a red sky in the west you thought of that white church steeple, the hills and Aunt Rose, God rest her soul.

Nostalgia Wins Friends: That's the kind of stuff eloquence is made of. When you tell of such thoughts you put feeling into them. These are the things you miss from your life of today. They have a pull because every listener had similar dreams. The account of your dreams reminds them of theirs. They have grown up, certainly, but they have never gotten over being those youngsters who dreamed, and imagined, and lived with fantasies.

Tell how you once told about your dream to Uncle Jeff and he laughed at you, even told your dad and mother that you'd be far better off without such crazy ideas. How dejected you felt after his laughing at you. But Aunt Sarah, Jeff's wife, told you to go on and dream. Young people were made to dream she said. "A teenager without dreams is nothing." She put her arm around you and said, "Grown-ups would never understand." It was no wonder that Aunt Sarah became your favorite aunt after that and you never cared much for Uncle Jeff.

Listeners Suffer with You: I heard a speaker use a story about one of his relatives laughing at a dream he had when he was a teen. Then he explained why such ridicule is wrong. A youngster needs assurance—not ridicule. The speaker used it as an appeal for the group to volunteer as Big Brothers. The boys needing Big Brothers had no fathers and the youngster needed someone he could admire and talk to who would encourage him. You can see the appeal in this device. Every man feels that he would like to do something to help, he feels that he has something for the youngster to admire, he asks, "What's holding me back?"

All Applaud Good Works: A friend tells you about a Bible class he runs at the Reformatory. He says, "Those boys come from broken homes. They surely appreciate my taking the time to go out there and work with them." The listener gets the thought, "Why don't I do something like that?"

The comedian asked, when his partner doubted a statement of his Baron Munchausen character, "Was you there, Charlie?" When you tell of your experiences, you were there. And your presence on the scene makes the incident much more real to the listener. You saw, heard, you reacted, and in retelling the incident you show how you feel about it.

Reading Produces Ideas: This morning in the mail you get a circular. The headline informs you, "You may already have won one of these $10,000 prizes." You react, "The dirty crooks, do they expect me to believe that?" You know that some of the more gullible will react in a different way, "Oh gee, such good luck, wait till I tell Penny." Everything you read will not stir your feelings like the line quoted, but some of your reading will. For you will learn of good movements, dedication, sacrifices, bad movements, boondoggling, tax wasting activities. All can arouse your emotions. Such ideas can come from any reading.

Ideas Are Everywhere in Print: Look for them in your newspapers, magazines, trade papers. There is gold in such printed pages, a quote from a news story, a columnist, an editorial, the sports pages, the cartoons, a headline in the news, or in an advertisement. Make notes of thoughts with which you agree or disagree. Cultivate the note habit and you'll never want for ideas to help inspire others.

Read the Holy Bible: Perhaps the most-popular source of ideas for eloquence is the Holy Bible. Shakespeare put it, "The Devil can cite scripture to his purpose." Without doubt you remember many verses and ideas from your Sunday School days. Those quotes might be familiar to your listeners. Read one page of the Bible, either from the Old or New Testament and you'll get ideas that show why the orators turn to it for material.

Great Ideas Come from Books: In his inaugural address President John Kennedy used the line, "Ask not what your country can do for you, ask what you can do for your country."

In a few days you knew that reading had turned up that line.

Scholars began to tell when it had been used before and who wrote it.

But the scholars hadn't used it in a speech to which millions were listening. You may never have an audience that large, but J.F.K. pointed out one place where ideas can be found.

You Gain by Being Receptive: When I find an item in my reading that I might use, I make a note of it, then add my thoughts on how I might use it. Here is a story I read–(Note I've cut out the words that might not be too good for speaking.)

> A little girl, nine years old, was in an orphanage. It was a nice orphanage, but that didn't help the little girl who needed affection. Two little old ladies ran the orphanage; they were kind but very strict, and mighty curious. The orphanage was shut off from the road by a high brick wall. The little ladies had good eyes and one day from an upstairs window they saw the little girl climb a tree by the wall and climb out on a branch above the wall. As they watched she put something in a fork in the tree and then she climbed down. Later the ladies took a light ladder and put it against the tree. One of them climbed up above the wall, reached out and took an envelope from the fork in the tree. They came back to the house, shut the door of their office, and together they opened the envelope. They took out a piece of ruled paper and on it they read, "Whoever you are, I love you."

Here are some points I thought I might make with the story–

We all need affection.

We are all ready to give affection if we are encouraged.

How long has it been since you told a loved one you loved him or her?

You may think of other points that this story will help you make. Listeners can feel for the little girl and they can appreciate her intimate feelings about needing someone to love and to return that love. The "How Long" question shows how each listener can be made a part of the story. The note shows how the little girl felt. Your question indicates that the listeners may be lax.

Reference Books Offer Ideas: I use the familiar quotation books a lot. If the subject of my speech is "It Pays to Dream," I look in the subject index and find over seventy offerings on dreams. Out of that number I should find one or more I can use. I combine the ones I select with my own ideas and I usually have a wealth of material. Reading the quotations sparks ideas. For instance, consider this line of Jean De La Fontaine (1621-1695):

> Beware as long as you live judging people by appearances.

What ideas does that thought bring to you?

Poetry Fits In Well: You may say, "I was never much for poetry." But is that true? You probably remember many lines from the poets you studied in high school. You may wonder why these lines stayed with you, because you did not specialize in literature. You never made a good grade in it. But the quotes stuck. Your memory brings back lines like—

> "Breathes there a man with soul so dead—"
> or,
> "We shall rest and faith, we shall need it—"
> or,
> "For all sad words of tongue or pen, the saddest are these,
> 'It might have been.' "

You may not recall the names of the authors, or poems from which these quotes came. But the lines have stayed with you through the years. Your listeners know these or similar lines. Quoting the lines gives you another connection with them. I used one of Eddie Guest's bits in a speech, and after the meeting a listener asked, "Do you use much poetry?" I told her that I used about one or two in a speech at the most. "It is like bringing in a witness to testify for you, isn't it?" she asked. I report the questions to indicate that many listeners like poetry and they think better of you if you use some of it.

Speaker's Aides Spark Ideas: I subscribe to a pocket-size magazine *Quote* that sends me 24 pages of ideas each week. Subjects are listed alphabetically. It is published by Public

Speakers Press, Anderson, S.C. 29621. *Quote* has given me ideas to use, or has sparked ideas that I have used. Another plus of such an aid is that it comes every week. I formed the habit of reading through one issue before the next one came. That keeps speech material on my mind. When I read an idea I might use, I make a note of it.

BORROW FROM THE ORATORY OF OTHERS

There is no need to repeat what the orator said in his words. Listen to his technique. Recordings of inspirational speeches can indicate the type of material that might work for you. The speaker's technique will show you how to use it. Recently I ran three inspirational recordings just to refresh my memory on the kind of material others use, and here is what I have noted. You were advised to–

control your mind
think positively
believe in yourself, your idea, your cause
think right about the possibilities of your job
set goals for yourself
have faith in yourself
use your imagination
work–do more than you are expected to do
try a new idea–test it
act like the success you want to be

You may say, "Why that's advice that I've heard ever since I was old enough to listen." It is that. And such advice has been given by the eloquent from the start of time. It is good because the listeners know that these are the things they should do.

Those same recordings gave this advice on things not to do–

don't worry
fear anything
be narrow minded
avoid pettiness
be a quitter
do a sloppy job on anything

There were these truths with which we agree–

> no stairway to the stars
> people are basically good
> the secret of success is *You*
> all improvement is self-improvement
> as you sow so shall you reap
> ask and you shall receive, seek and you shall find,
> knock and it will be opened up to you
> as you believe so shall it be
> to get anything, you have to work for it
> only 5% of us are successes.

Think how you can use that 5% idea–Stop drifting and where do you wind up? Closer to that 5% that is up at the top.

Let This Quote Spark Your Thinking: The speaker states, "My company bought a million dollar computer. It is a giant machine that would fill every cubic foot of this hall. But you know something? It can't do one simple problem until a man, girl or small boy feeds it something."

Think a minute on that idea. It says that the human being is needed, a man, girl or small boy is needed. Without the human being the machine is nothing. Thus a human being is more important than any machine man can imagine.

How to Fit the Idea to Your Story: Your company perhaps is never going to invest in a million dollar computer. Here's a way I heard that "machine vs. human" idea used. The speaker told about a forty thousand dollar machine that his boss had bought to help increase production. The boss was particularly proud of that machine. Every day he walked out of his handsome office and down the factory aisle to look at his pride and joy. The big man watched the machine operate, he put his ear close to it and listened to it, he was even seen to take out his handkerchief and brush a speck of dust off the machine. On the path of his daily trip to that machine he passed ten to twelve workmen. He didn't even bother to speak to one of them. Yet he was paying any one of those men more than the interest charges on the loan to buy that machine. The speaker concluded, "If I had mentioned the fact that the workmen were more important, the boss would have said, 'Workmen, huh, are a dime a dozen, but machines like this are out of this world.' Yet even his lowest paid workman was costing him more in pay and benefits than the big machine was costing him." The speaker was making the point that if the employer can't see the importance of human relations, that importance can be spelled out in dollars and cents.

Study Both Words and Emotions. My notes on what orators said in recordings, shows how a bit of listening sparks ideas. Listening gives you more than reading because you see how the speakers put feeling into the words. Look for both the ideas and the feeling put into expressing them.

The Material of Eloquence Is Easy to Find: You walk along the busy street. A man in front of you staggers and falls. Ten or twelve people walk on, some walk around him. One stops, bends over, tries to give him some help. You have walked by, but now you stop, tell yourself, "What the heck?" you turn and walk back to see if you can do anything.

That paragraph gives you a thought, right? That's why I suggest you start with these devices–

your experiences
your reading–newspaper, magazine,
reference books, poetry
the oratory of others–if a speech on TV arouses your feelings, it may furnish an eloquent idea for you. If you feel that a recording tells it like it is, some of its ideas might be of use to you.

Notes Help You Remember: Notes have been mentioned a number of times. The eloquent make notes. Make a note of a shoeshine boy selling football pool cards. Note all that happened in the exchange between you and him, then note where you think the profit on the cards goes, and what the criminal element might be doing with that money. Now you have something to cause you to burn and to rail at the authorities for allowing such things to run openly in your town. Couldn't you work up a storm over this situation. Such storms bring on eloquence. Make notes of some of your thoughts at the time. Report how you feel at the time you make the note and the idea will be more useful when you start putting your speech together. Some notes you may never use, but those you do use will save time for you.

13

A PLAN FOR DEVELOPING ELOQUENT UNITS

Successful speakers handle their eloquence in units. A unit might be considered as a short speech—three minutes, five minutes or longer. You first state your premise, second, bring on your evidence, and third, restate your premise. Here is a formula to build such a unit:

FORMULA FOR A PRESENTATION UNIT

1. Get a presentation idea.
2. Use the idea to build your case.
3. Tell why listeners should be interested, and what they gain by going along.
4. Explain how they can help.

1. Get a Presentation Idea

A presentation idea might be called window dressing. But it helps. It tells the listener that you have done your homework. A presentation based on facts alone can be eloquent, but it doesn't have as much power as one that arouses the listeners' emotions, on a point with which they agree or disagree. The extra something might be a picture, the report of a conversation, a line of poetry, or a heroic story. You have your subject–now look for the best tools to help you arouse the listener's emotion.

Let's say you start, "Yesterday in the court house across the square an eighteen year old boy, Joseph Jeri, was sentenced by Judge Broom to life imprisonment. Four years ago that boy graduated from the eighth grade of Gravely School with the highest grades in his class. What happened to the boy in those four years? I'm going to try to answer that question because similar things are happening to too many promising boys. That boy had no father, his mother had to work to help support her other five children and couldn't give him the attention he needed. If he had had a Big Brother through those years perhaps the story would be different."

On the same plea, you might have said, "Just this last year 24 boys, teenagers from that neighborhood, have been in trouble with the police."

These two ideas follow the plan of presenting a problem, or a number of problems, and then presenting your remedy, that tells listeners what they can do today to help solve the problem.

Shaping an Idea: You see a photograph in the morning newspaper. A statue of a great General has been knocked off its pedestal in the town square. Now it lies broken in a pile of rubble. The head is separated from the body, the arms and legs were nearby, a rat was sniffing at a hand. That is the picture. What idea does it give you?

My first thought was–

"What does it profit a man?"

Next–"Hero today, goat tomorrow."

Then–"Fame is fickle."

Such ideas add a bit of color to an eloquent bit. "One minute on the top of the world, the next flat and broken in the gutter." The listener says, "So true."

How This Idea Was Used: I heard this idea used at a retirement party. The executive who was retiring had spent thirty years working to build his department. He had just listened to a number of speeches that complimented his contributions to the company over the years. He said,

"Let me start by saying that I have enjoyed every minute of my association with you. Tonight you have been kind enough to praise my accomplishments. But, you know, those accomplishments are yours as much as mine. I am leaving now and I won't be able to help any more. But let's keep this thought in mind." (The lights went out and the picture of the fallen General amidst the rubble flashed on a lighted screen.) There was a moment of silence. Then the speaker went on, "We have worked hard and long to build this company. Let's dedicate ourselves to keeping on with our building so that never in my time or yours will we see our accomplishments shattered into rubble because of our neglect." End of speech.

The guests put a lot of feeling into the applause at that bit of eloquence. They knew that the guest of honor felt as they did about the company. To emphasize that fact he had given them something they would remember for a long time.

How to Develop Your Idea: Most ideas you find can be developed to help prove your case. Here is an example–

In Chapter 12 I quoted a poem by Jean De La Fontaine. The quote was, "Beware as long as you live of judging people by appearances." I had never heard of this poet before. I had never read the quote, but there is an idea there. What do you think of this–(Make the quote.) Then say,

"That same warning applies to projects. To hear the proponents describe this plan you could assume we are getting something for nothing. But let's look a bit closer–"

(Now you bring on all of your negatives.)

Next you ask listeners to think, to analyze, as you have.

The quote could be used by the opposite side.

"That same warning applies to projects. This proposal looks good, doesn't it? It looks almost too good. I was against it at first, but I studied it from every angle and asked myself, 'How wrong can I be?' This deal is good. Just think what we get–

(Now list the benefits, then add–)

It looks good, it is good, I move we accept it."

Speak those words with feeling and you have created a bit of eloquence.

Daily Life Is Full of Ideas: The blind man, who runs the newspaper stand, in the friendly store on your bus corner, always has a cheery word for everybody. He is laughing at his handicap and spreading his good humor to others who might be considered more fortunate than he. Each day as you move about your duties, you encounter other such characters. Many can help you build an eloquent bit. Observe and you can find many such ideas.

2. Build Your Case Around the Idea

The idea is a vehicle on which to load your evidence. Make a list of the factors that will help the listener agree. Write down every thought. If you are for the project, make a list similar to this–

Assume Listeners Are on the Side of–God–Country–law–order–truth–virtue–honesty–peace–plenty–equality–love of neighbor–fairness–harmony–self-respect–courtesy. Add other similar factors to your list. All are associated with the good things in life. If you are against, make a list similar to this–

Assume Listeners Are Against–regulation–oppression–bureaucracy–dictatorship–red-tape–mob rule–tyranny–crime–treason–racketeering–war–cheating–lying–deception–noise-pollution–All these things are associated with the bad side of life.

These lists may be too large to use in any speech. I suggest listing everything so that you won't miss an important factor. Then select from your list three or four of the evils or advantages you want to present. You may have fourteen but the listener will do a better job of remembering three or four. Select the three or four that you feel will have the strongest appeal to the group.

Working Up Your Data: In the chapter before I mentioned the shoeshine boy in the office lobby trying to sell you a football card. Later in the small smoke shop you heard a friend place a bet on a horse. Then last week the police picked up a young man at the high school. They thought he was pushing drugs. They found no drugs on him or in his car, but in the trunk of the car he had over 300 football pool tickets.

You see nothing wrong about the football tickets or the betting on the horses, but that drug thing is serious. You feel men who would start teenagers on drugs are the scum of the earth. Buying a football pool ticket or putting up a bet is putting money into the pockets of this scum. The shoeshine boy sees nothing wrong in selling the pool cards, the cigar store man in taking the bets. But the end result of the activities is the money that allows the racketeer to try to start teenagers on drugs. You have a strong case here, for many of your listeners may buy football tickets, many may place bets on horses, but they never have thought of the drug trade that their small change helps finance. But if that is the end result of buying the football tickets, the listeners can stop buying them. You might quote one of the bettors, "This guy's been my bookie for years and now the police have him up for selling drugs. If I have been helping finance that drug trade, I can stop it right now."

As you read through this analysis, you perhaps think of other arguments you feel more potent than the ones mentioned. Substitute your thoughts because without doubt you can show more feeling when you speak about your thoughts.

3. Show Why They Should Be Interested

Listeners are continually asking, "What does this mean to me?" In the drug example they feel they know. But if your appeal is for a project or plan, tell them specifically what benefits will accrue to them. Make a list similar to this one—

> accomplishment—money—health—family—praise—virtue—love of fellowman—good citizenship—standing up to be counted—brotherhood—intelligence—fellowship.

Don't Assume They Know, Tell Them: You may feel that some of your benefits are so well known that they need no mentioning. But take no chance, explain your point. You say he will save money. Ok, how will he save, how much? Have him asking, "You mean I'll save ten bucks?" The fault of most speakers is in assuming that the listener understands and doesn't need to be told. Don't take any chances, tell him fully.

4. Explain How They Can Help

This is the button-up of your eloquent unit. It should be the easiest part you work out. You want him to–

write respresentatives in Congress
talk to neighbors
explain a brochure
sign a petition
ask for a donation.

You knew this objective when you started to build the talk. Be specific in what you want the group to do and how. Tell the listeners in a way they understand. Don't allow them to say, "He told us why we should fight this idea, but he didn't tell us how."

Most Listeners Want to Help: Assume that they want to do what you ask because they always do their share. You have pointed out how they can help. You know they are right-thinking. Then they surely should enlist. I heard a speaker ask a group, "You want this campaign to be a success, don't you?" Then as the listeners considered the question, he paused. Heads all over the room nodded agreement. Some speakers go so far as to start the nodding. When they want the group to nod, they nod as they ask the question. One speaker who needed workers for a fund drive for his church said, "A friend told me he hadn't voted at the last election, 'What does one vote mean?' he asked." Now the speaker cited cases where one vote decided elections. Then he added, "And one worker counts too. None of us want somebody else doing what we should do. You are important, make one solicitation and you will see how important you are."

Making the task seem easy

No listener wants to write 10 letters or make 20 calls. I heard one speaker tell his group of solicitors, "This telephone call has been made easy for you. What you say when your prospect answers the phone is on this little card. The prospect's name and telephone number are on one side, the request to make on the other side. You don't need to memorize it, just read it. How much time does it take to make that call? Let's check and find out." With that he had a member of the group make a call while listeners checked their watches. When the call was completed he asked how long it took. The time was less than two minutes. "That's what we want from each of you, three of those calls, six minutes of your time. Is that too much to ask for a project as worthwhile as this?" If the task seems easy, you'll get more volunteers.

Explain Why "Do It Now" Is Important: Most workers are inclined to stall before they start any solicitation. Show why it pays to start now. I heard a fund raiser say, "We'll all be home by nine pm. When you get there, go straight to the telephone and call your first prospect. Don't wait until tomorrow or the next day, do it now."

Offer a Choice: If there is more than one way to do what you want, mention both. But don't use more than two. Then emphasize that the worker is to do this or this. One listener may prefer one way over the other, and may move in faster if you don't insist he do it your way.

Mention Their Possible Loss: When the listener will lose something if the activity doesn't succeed, stress that. All of us fear losing anything. To induce a group of neighbors to attend a city council meeting and protest a zoning change, one speaker said, "If council votes this change, we'll have stores and small manufacturing plants in this beautiful residential neighborhood. Do we want that?" The speaker knew the answer, and he had a capacity crowd at the council meeting.

Ask for action positively

Ask for action as if you expected to get it. In your asking picture yourself as a hero, a leader, the kind of individual we all admire. Ask in a half-hearted way and you will not succeed. Too many speakers make a brilliant plea for their causes. They persuade the listeners that they should do something but don't tell them what to do and how to do it. Tell your listeners and you'll get more of the kind of action you want.

CHECK THE UNIT FOR APPEAL

When you have your unit finished, check to see if you have used the three tools of eloquence—

1. Have you shown how strongly you feel?
2. Have you appealed to the listener's wants and desires?
3. Is the wording the strongest you can use?

Small changes in any of these tools can strengthen your appeal.

START WITH A SMALL UNIT

The unit idea allows you to experiment at being eloquent. Work up a three-minute unit on some cause you feel about. Follow the four step formula in building it. When you get a chance try it on a group. Note which units accomplish their purpose. Try to develop at least one unit for each speech. Some speakers may be born eloquent, but the speakers that seem most eloquent for causes have taken time to get themselves steamed up about the good they are doing.

PREPARATION A CONTINUOUS PROCESS

Let's assume that ever since you took your job ten years ago you have been irritated at the way your boss talks to the help. His verbal treatment indicates they are all slaves. You can't say much about it while you are working for him, but someday you mean to make an eloquent talk on how to handle the people supervised. Stories of his ineptness will give you material. Ok, start making notes of those mistakes now. Start a file folder on "Courtesy" and put all the notes of these mistakes in it. File in the same folder any quotes, poems, pictures or other data on the subject that you come across. When you start to prepare your speech on "Courtesy" you'll have a fat folder of ideas. The procedure is close to what the professional speaker follows when he agrees to talk on a subject. The speech you hear tonight may have been started years ago. An incident was observed, a note was made, and the note joined other notes in a folder taken out of the file when the speaker started to organize the talk. Without the notes the preparation would have been more of a chore. With them the human interest items flashed back before the speaker's memory. The problem became more of arrangement than writing. Get in the habit of filing speech material in a way that makes it easily available when you need it. The habit will help you make better speeches.

NOTE HOW THIS FITS THE UNIT FORMULA

Let's examine this procedure to see how it can be compared to the formula given at the start of the chapter.

1. *Get a Presentation Idea:* You have selected "Courtesy." Why? There is too little of it in the business world today.

2. *Use the Idea to Build Your Case:* Arrange your notes on instances of discourtesy so that you start with small offenses and then those that build up in importance. Ask what they would want to do if they were the victims. Show your disgust at the offender and your sympathy and compassion for the ones stepped on.

3. *Tell Why the Listeners Should Be Interested:* Courtesy pays. It makes life easier for all. Picture the difference between the office where courtesy rules and where everybody feels downtrodden. Courtesy gets jobs done. We all work better and faster for the one who treats us as an equal. Ask how they feel when they are treated discourteously, how they feel about the guilty party.

4. *Explain How They Can Help:* Ask them to start tomorrow with a smile, a friendly greeting for all. Suggest they use, "please" and "thank you" more often.

The formula works rather well, doesn't it? Try it on your next speech.

14

HOW TO USE YOUR ELOQUENCE

"Eloquence is difficult for the listener to take."

"Eloquence takes too much out of you."

Students of public speaking have made these statements to me. Both are true.

A speaker should understand these two facts. Let's say you plan a ten-minute speech on a cause. Don't try to be eloquent for the whole ten minutes. The most experienced orator might have difficulty carrying such a load. In your ten minutes, plan four eloquent units of perhaps one minute each.

HOW THE ELOQUENT DO IT

Start your speech with an eloquent unit that indicates you are serious about this cause. Lift listeners up on your cloud. Then bring them back to reality with facts and figures. Now take them for the second ride into the wild, blue yonder. Next soothe them with your factual material. When you have them relaxed, lift them again, hold them up a short time, then bring them down. Try to finish with your most eloquent unit. Make it ask for action. This outline gives you a pattern that is sure fire.

LET LISTENERS LIKE YOUR PLAN

You have heard would-be orators who took you up on cloud nine and kept you there too long. The plan to sway you took on the sound of haranguing, pleading, begging. When they brought you back to reality, you were exhausted. Your desire to pick up your banner and follow the leader had somewhat cooled. If the speaker had given you a break now and then as this plan does, more listeners would have gone along. You have heard speakers that were mighty eloquent at the start of a speech, then used no eloquence as they went on. It seemed as if they had lost some of their enthusiasm for their project. Realize that too much eloquence may tire the listener, and sprinkle your emotional bits throughout your speech.

Fit to You: Do only what you feel you can do. I heard a teacher tell his speaking class, "Get down on your knees, let large tears run down your face, use your handkerchief to dry your tears, let your voice show your anguish, reach out to them–appeal, appeal." The teacher knew that most of his group would say, "I never could go that far." His answer was, "Ok, come as close to that intensity as you can." That's good advice. You are trying to show your feeling, and if you feel ridiculous trying to shed tears before a group, the group will sense that and perhaps shed a few tears for you. If you can wave your arms, jump around and shout without feeling ridiculous, do that. But you can be eloquent standing still and speaking in almost whispers. Here is an exercise that allows you to check on how well you display your feelings when you say meaningful words. (Note that no violent exercise is called for.)

The Exercise

Stand in front of a large mirror, hands in front of you, raised just below shoulders, palms open, fingers spread. Now say slowly with a slight pause between each word, "I was amazed (pause,) bewildered (pause) dumbfounded." Did your hands move? Did your face take on a puzzled expression?

Try the exercise again. Say the same words. Let your hands move naturally, let your mouth drop open, let your face show your emotion.

Use these words in your speech and show how you felt. Listeners would hear the words, they would see the effect on your emotions. Wouldn't some of them ask, "If things are that bad, shouldn't I do something to help?"

Truths Make Good Relief: For relief between the eloquent units, use truths we all accept. Use one like, "That was the thought that guided our founding fathers." The listeners come down to earth. They agree with the thought, "It was, wasn't it?" Fill in with facts, testimonials, figures, data to help relieve the tension you have produced with your oratory. Perhaps your eloquent proposal might be interpreted as tilting at windmills. Temper that with questions like–

"Who can say this won't work?"

"Who knows a better way?"

"They laughed at Robert Fulton, didn't they?"

Use the spaces in between your oratorical units to help build your case. Bring on a visual, read a clipping from a newspaper, use an audience participation stunt. Then when you feel the group is relaxed, bring on your next eloquent unit.

Assign Objectives to Each Bit: There is little sense in swaying an audience just to show your power over them. You want your unit of eloquence to recruit them to your way of thinking or to agree to take some action. Let them know why you feel as you do. Your objective is to win the listener to your side. Don't forget that. Don't tell them, "I am going to sell you." Their answer would probably be, "You and who else?" Persuade them with your appeal. You know how you feel when the fat guy in the cigar commercial says, "Try one and we've got you." No one wants to be got, and all resist being sold. Do you admit you were ever sold anything? A better approach is asking–

"Let's reason this out–"

"Let's look at the facts."

"Can you see any fault in this reasoning?"

Then let you facts convince listeners why they should go along with you.

Honesty Pays Off: Don't waste eloquence on phony causes. If you don't believe in the idea, don't try to get eloquent on it. Listeners sense any deceit. There is no profit in telling the group that a task will be easy if it is difficult. They know any extra work will not be easy. Ok, tell them it will be difficult and they will go along with your honesty. Use, "It will be difficult, yes, but you can do it." If you feel that some of your statements are too strong, revise them. You've heard speakers go so far overboard in their statements that you lost faith in their truthfulness. You gain nothing by making the listener say, "You could sell ice to the Esquimaux." You want them to say,

"You make sense."

"You have an idea."

"Why shouldn't I help?"

Slower Delivery Is Insurance: If you speak fast, a rather high percentage of your listeners may not hear exactly what you say. When you tell what you want, slow up. Say,

"You are asked to give just ten minutes of your time."

Study the faces as you speak. If they show that any statement is not quite understood, repeat it thus,

"That's right–just ten minutes of your time."

Remember that numbers are difficult to hear. You say, "Two," and the listener may hear "Three." "When you say "Two Dollars" put the emphasis on the number. "Dollars" is a two-syllable word and is more easily heard than the number. The listener hears the "dollars" but not how many.

Use the pause, and during it check the faces for understanding. The same pause can tell you how well your plea is accepted.

Every group is made up of individuals with varying IQs. Don't be content because you feel the more intelligent hear and understand. How about those not so blessed? By slowing up you may reach them too. Let's assume you are speaking at your normal speed. What happens when you slow up? The listener gives you closer attention. You are giving what you say more importance. He doesn't want to miss anything important. Try this slowing up device on one sentence. Speak a bit louder and as distinctly as possible. The effect on your listeners will show why the eloquent use such devices.

Key Words or Lines Go Better if Memorized: Memorize your key lines so that you will say them right. If you are using a bit of popular poetry the extra work will help you get it right. When you memorize what the great man said, get it right. I use a device that works well. I type the quotation on a small card, pull it from my pocket and read the line. The use of the card gives the listener something to watch and a pause that lets him consider the thought. The same advice applies to choice bits you create. Get them in the best words for speaking and memorize them. Your memorized phrase will be said with better timing. It will express more conviction.

Rehearse Important Words and Lines: Practice saying them again and again. Learn to put the emphasis where it belongs. Speak the words aloud instead of reading them. You are interested in how they sound to others. On lines you compose yourself, check to see that they are in the best words for speaking. For instance, you know the line—

1. "He travels the fastest who travels alone."

   That thought could be expressed—

2. "Travel alone and you'll go the fastest."

One of the two wordings will speak better for you. Say each aloud and decide which you speak better. Both have the same number of words. Number one is a well-known line of Kipling's that many listeners will know, but which line rolls easier off your tongue. In this type of rehearsal a tape recorder can help you choose the best for you. If you are trying to warn the group of what the enemy might do to them and you plan to use a word to ridicule the enemy such as *contemptible,* rehearse saying that word, trying to make it sound as corrupt and shameless as you can. This is the type of word you might stumble over if you say it too fast.

Humor Is Your Enemy: Beware of that flash of wit. When you are asking listeners to consider a serious problem, to shed tears for some unfortunates, make a sacrifice, dig a bit deeper, get involved, that bright wisecrack that pops into your head can kill the mood. The purpose of much eloquence is to move the listeners towards doing or giving. Your wisecrack may get a laugh but it breaks any spell you may have created. Listeners' thoughts of what might be done fly away with that laugh. They may not want to think about victims, unfortunates or injustices, but they do enjoy a laugh. You want action and a laugh may lose it for you. If you can kid about your subject, why should the listener take it seriously?

BEWARE OF MUCH TOO MUCH

Shakespeare put it, "More than a little may be much too much." In eloquence you are asking listeners to feel with you, suffer with you, be enthusiastic with you, and do what you ask. All through the chapter I have stressed the advice, "Be moderate." They can take only so much, you can give only so much. You want results, not what Aesop called, "Much outcry and little outcome."

A TIME TO BE CREATIVE

In using eloquence you have to be. All of the devices suggested in these chapters ask you to create. You–

dress up your own thoughts.
borrow and make changes to fit your theme.
quote and add your interpretation.

Arrange the words so that you can put more feeling in them. Let you feelings show, express your faith and listeners will rate you as eloquent.

When someone compliments you on your eloquence say, "Thanks, but anyone can get eloquent on–

this cause
this subject
this leader

Anyone can, if he is sincere."

Part Three

HOW TO GET HUMOR OR ELOQUENCE WITH ANY SPEECH DEVICE

The most popular speech devices of successful speakers are—

- the anecdote
- people, characters
- conversation
- news
- possessions
- statistics, figures
- visuals
- dramatics
- audience participation

The chapters in this part of the book give ideas on how each of these speaking devices can be used to get the result you want—the humor or eloquence.

15

THE ANECDOTE IS NUMBER ONE

For humor–

For eloquence–

The story is the speaker's most useful tool.

It brightens dull material.

It gets attention fast.

It holds attention.

It brings back attention.

Go on, add to that list.

Most of us think about the story as the gag type that the boss hears at the bowling alley and brings back to the office. It is great for those quick laughs, of course. But my statement includes the kind of story that doesn't try for laughs.

STORIES HELP PERSUADE

How about the story the speaker uses to persuade your service club to support a summer camp for kids from the ghetto? He builds his case with stories about the benefits to those kids. Then how about the salesman who tells you about a customer that didn't think his product would help, but the doubter bought it, used it, and now he is enthusiastic about it fulfilling the claims? That's persuasion, isn't it? And it is in story form. A speaker can hold interest with stories of benefits, when data or figures or facts on the same benefits may leave listeners cold. The anecdote can be humorous or eloquent. The result depends on the job you want it to do.

STORIES HELP AROUSE EMOTION

One of my friends wrote a book on how to speak in public. In it he stated that he did not use stories. He is a popular speaker and is much in demand at meetings of trade associations. I knew he held interest with his efforts. If he did it without stories, I wondered what new secret he had discovered. A short time later when I heard him talk I found he had no big secret weapon. He told fourteen anecdotes in a twenty-minute talk. He used no joke stories, he talked about his family, his boss, business associates, taxi drivers. Some of the anecdotes got laughs, some excited sympathy, but every story helped make a point. I remember one story he told about a factory in his town closing and throwing 120 men out of jobs. He talked of the lost jobs, the 500 men, women, and children without income, the inability of the town to furnish the jobs needed to put those people back to work, the lack of welfare people to take care of food, the red-tape, frustrations, despair. He aroused the group's feelings with that recital. There is not a laugh in such a story, but there are many angles to call for eloquence. With him the point illustrated by the story was the important thing. He put his material in story form because he knew that listeners liked to listen to stories.

HOW TO WORK IN THE FUNNY STORY

How do you profit by telling a gag story you heard a TV comedian use last week? Many of the listeners heard the comedian tell it, and he no doubt told it better than you can. But if the gag will emphasize the point you want to make, tell it. Let's assume the story is about a fellow who stubbed his toe, tell your story and get your laugh. Then tie it into your subject with a line like, "And aren't we about to stub our toes if we don't move ahead on this proposal?"

THE FAMILIAR STORY GIVES YOU INSURANCE

Some gag stories you use will be ones that many of the listeners have heard. Such a story has a better chance of registering than one new to them. You start, "Last week we heard Pete Whosis tell this story on TV." A smile will light the faces of those who listen to Pete. Others will snap to attention to hear what they missed. They will rate you as one of them, you listen to Pete. Pete's story is only a break for relief if you don't help make your point. Use it to emphasize a point and you have scored twice.

STORIES OF WHAT HAPPENS TO YOU GO BETTER

Most of the stories you hear in public speeches are accounts of the speaker's experiences. The story is told exactly as it happened, or changed in detail here and there to make the story serve the speaker's purpose. A young woman in my speech class told me, "I have trouble getting my group to listen to advice." I suggested that the speaker build success stories around his advice. The giver of un-asked-for advice can't win a popularity contest because advice indicates that the speaker knows more than the receiver. For this reason the speaker does better by telling a story of what Sammy or Mamie Blow did, and how the third party's plan worked out. For instance—

HERE'S HOW TO ROLL YOUR OWN

"My friend Sammy Blow was watching the card game at Bachelor Hall when the players took a dollar out of the pot to finance a pail of beer. A player got the pail and picked up the dollar.

"Sammy asked, 'You guys pay a dollar to fill that pail?'

"They admitted they did.

" 'I'll bet you a quarter apiece that I can get it filled for fifty cents.'

"The bet was made and Sammy started off with a pail and a witness. At the B and G he laid the pail on the bar and asked the bartender, 'Can you get fifty cents worth of beer into that?'

"The bartender examined the pail and allowed he could. 'Don't fill it too full, I don't want to spill it on my way back,' Sammy said."

MOVE OUT OF THE HERO'S ROLE

In telling this story note that the speaker used the bit of advice given in Chapter 5, he didn't make himself the wise one. Don't say, "I've tried it this way and it is easier." Tell how another tried the new way with success. Quote what the speaker said about the method. Then suggest, "Why not try it and see if it works for you?"

STATEMENTS, CLAIMS, EVIDENCE ARE MORE PALATABLE IN STORY FORM

Your back-up data holds more interest when you build a story around it. And stories are not too difficult to find. No matter what you do or say there is a story in it. You claim your plan will save time. Ok, how can you prove it? The easiest way is to build a story about how the plan was used by another and how much time it saved. By this slight change, you put your proof in the most interesting form for your listener.

You tell how Chuck Jarvis said the plan would not work when you told him about it.

He said, "I know it won't work, but just to prove it won't I'll try it. I'll give it a fair trial too."

Ok, you got the basis of drama here, antagonism, struggle. The man is trying the plan, not to save labor, but to prove that it won't save labor.

He tries the plan. He finds it does save labor. He says, "I never would have believed it. Boy have we got something here."

From antagonism to enthusiasm in one short story. If the listeners know Chuck, and know how reluctant he is to try anything new, it is a better story and much better proof.

FORGET THE HARD WAY–PUT IT IN A STORY

Any speaker can explain a plan, list the reasons why it is good, quote figures with logic and common sense, but it is better persuasion to allow a third party to testify to such benefits. The story offers a vehicle that allows the presentation of facts in a way the listener likes and readily accepts. Listeners are less likely to say, "I'd like somebody to try that on my boss." If the speaker brings on a number of witnesses listeners are more likely to say, "Maybe I oughta give it a try."

EVERYBODY, EVERYTHING MAKES STORY MATERIAL

This morning I backed the car out of my driveway and Mrs. Hegarty reminded me of the neighbor's car parked on the boulevard. Down at the corner, a STOP street, a joker ploughed right thru without stopping. At the four-way stop, another of his kind seemed to be going to a fire. Every light I came to turned red just as I reached it. At the parkig lot the attendant sold me a chance on a car. One buck gone over the hill for a cause I may not have approved. All that in seven minutes. I could say, "I drove down town and nothing happened." But things did happen, and these things make stories that are good speech material. The experienced speaker manufactures stories out of what happened, and his thoughts on what happened. Try doing the same and your speeches will pick up in interest.

SAVE WORK BY GETTING THE MEAT FIRST

A most successful speaker told me this, "Get the meat for the talk first, then think of stories to brighten it up." He has an idea. First he makes an outline of the points he wants to make, then the arguments on each point. This gives him a clear picture of where he needs some life. Now he looks for stories to brighten up his presentation. This is the reverse of the plan of looking for stories first. As you study the points you want to make, stories will come to you. It may be a story you haven't thought of in years. It may be one that the boss told you that morning. It may be a thought, an experience that came as you worked over your points. But stories will come just as they did on that ride down town.

THE POINT GIVES THE STORY VALUE

My thought is that unless your story helps you make your point, it is better to forget it. Tell a story that has nothing to do with your point and what have you gained? Perhaps a laugh.

But unless your objective is to make the group laugh, you have not advanced your purpose. The story you heard the other morning may be mighty funny. Instead of telling it for the laugh, try to tie it into what you are trying to prove. A few simple changes may help you come up with a story that focuses attention on the point you are trying to make. The next time you hear a funny story, think of what points you could make with it. Try that right now with this story:

Two girls walking on the streets in Chicago noticed a sailor behind them. "I believe that sailor is following us," one said.

"Let's turn a corner and see," said the other.

They turned one corner, then another, and then a third. The sailor still pursued them. Finally one of the girls went back to the sailor and said, "Sailor, you stop following us or go get another sailor."

I heard that story used to make the point, "The girl knew what she wanted." It could make the point, "The sailor wasn't properly prepared." What ones can you add to these two?

SIX TIPS THAT MAKE YOUR STORY-TELLING MORE EFFECTIVE

1. *Use to Make Your Evidence More Interesting:* Put your data and evidence in story form. The listener likes to listen to stories.

2. *Use to Bring On Third Parties:* You may say that the policy is right. But the listener asks, "Says who?" Answer them with stories of others who agree with you.

3. *Use People and Locations the Listener Knows:* Use locations they know, conditions under which they live. An elephant hunt in far away Africa may be interesting, but a fender-bumping argument down at the corner is something the listener can see, relate to and appreciate.

4. *Use Enough Time:* Don't rush your story. Give the listeners enough time to figure out what was said and who said it. They need time to understand the action.

5. *Don't Claim Too Much:* When you bring on a third party to give evidence, don't have the number three claim too much. Keep the claims reasonable. How do you feel about the joker who claims too much in the TV commercials?

6. *Emphasize Your Point:* Let the listener know why you told the story. If you think the idea is wrong, let Joe, Betty and Buster say why it is wrong. Then just to make sure, add, "If all of these people agree, this must be wrong."

USE "ONCE UPON A TIME–" MORE. LISTENERS LIKE STORIES

I asked a famous speaker, "Do you ever lose attention?"

"Oh, yes," he admitted, "in almost every speech. But I have a sure-fire device for getting it back. Just four words, "Once upon a time–"

You know that people like stories. Ok, why not put your humor and eloquence in story form?"

Use a story to get a laugh.

Use a story to arouse an emotion.

Use what the listeners want to get what you want.

16

CHARACTERS HELP BUILD EFFECTS

They are needed, just like in the play or the movie.

Talk about people and you can be—humorous or eloquent.

Some people are funny naturally. Others cry so for compassion or sympathy that a description of their plights arouses emotion in the listener.

Let's say you start your speech—

"Your chairman, Sam Stone, was my roommate at college. But we've made a deal—we agreed if he wouldn't tell you anything about me, I wouldn't tell you anything about him."

I heard a woman speaker use a variation of this. She said, "Your chairman married a girl friend of mine, and I know a lot about him."

You have heard this type of humor used many times with success. The bit gets a smile, and it brings the speaker closer to the group.

THERE IS HUMOR AND ELOQUENCE IN PEOPLE

To introduce your subject, you say—

"I told my wife that I was coming here to make a speech. She asked, 'What are you going to talk about?'

"I said, 'My subject is 'Law and Order.' "

She asked, "What do you know about law and order?"

That's an attempt at humor, isn't it? It goes better if you were introduced as a prominent lawyer or perhaps a judge.

The men in the group can appreciate this. They have wives too. Such an opening relates you to the listeners and it also gives you a chance to explain why you were speaking on this angle of law and order.

YOUR KIDS CAN HELP TOO

You might mention what your ten-year old son said when you told him you were going over to Canton to make a speech. He asked, "How long is this speech?"

You say, "About twenty minutes."

He then asked, "Mom, why would anyone want to listen to you for twenty minutes?"

You say, "I need that much time to tell the club why they should sponsor a boy's camp this year."

He answered, "If it's about the camp, I'd like to hear it. I could tell them a lot about that camp and what the kids think of it."

Now you say, "He could too, he's been to camp, played with the kids, worked on projects with them; he knows how they look forward to it. Follow this with descriptions of the ghetto backgrounds for three of the boys you want to send to summer camp. Then add, "Three hundred kids from the same kind of families will go to camp this summer if we help."

You have drifted from a humorous remark to a bit of eloquence in no time, haven't you? Your talk of people can help you start with either humor or eloquence.

NEIGHBORS, ASSOCIATES AND INNOCENT BYSTANDERS WANT TO HELP

It is better to use ordinary people than to try to show you are in contact with doctors, lawyers and merchant chiefs

Perhaps one or more of these biggies in the news is a friend of yours. But most of your listeners know no such great ones, and for that reason much of such talk sounds unreal. I heard one speaker say, "I had contact with this great man for years, I saw him regularly, talked to him often: I was important to him and you know why? (Pause)–I delivered his evening newspaper." After such an opening the speaker could quote his great man without the listener feeling that he was trying to be pretentious. Dropping names gets a speaker nowhere. Perhaps it has a sense of humor, for we laugh at a joker who tries to play up his importance. Listeners know the same kind of little people you know. Suppose you describe one of your associates at the office as, "He's one of these executives that ride a motorcycle." Only one who rides a motorcycle can understand the kind of fellow you mean. If nobody rides a motorcycle, they think they know. Use the boys in the shipping department, the women in central steno, the elevator operators. They are the type of people the listener knows and loves and talks to every day.

PEOPLE BRING FACTS TO LIFE

I heard a speaker ask, "What's happened to the expression, 'Your grandfadder's moustache.'?" Whenever I heard it I thought of the long handlebars my grandfather wore. But the expression is gone with change. Today it would be, "Your grandson's moustache." The speaker went on, "Last week my grandson, age 19, telephoned and asked if I'd be home for a few minutes. I told him I would. 'I got a big surprise for you,' he said. Well, I sat there thinking of what the surprise might be and how much it was going to cost me. As each thought came to me I said, 'Oh, no, not that.' That expression was still in order when he showed up with a budding moustache."

This type of trivia makes good speech material. The speaker's subject was. "We Resist Change." And so he illustrated his point by talking about the kind of people his listeners knew. Each of them knew a young whippersnapper who tried to grow a handlebar moustache.

HOW TO TALK ABOUT PEOPLE

Listeners rate you on the attitude you show in speaking

about and to the characters you use. Follow these cautions and you will make a better impression:

1. *Give the Character a Name:* He or she has one, so use it. If you don't know the name, invent one. A character seems more real with a name. Say, "We got a shipping clerk named Chuck Long. I claim Chuck is the greatest shipping clerk in the world. He can get shipments to places that aren't even on the map." In inventing a name forget any thought of comedy. If you called Chuck a name like Enscore Hooperdiddle, the listeners may wonder if they are supposed to laugh. Chuck Long sounds like the name of a good guy who might pass the collection plate in your church.

2. *Make the Character Important:* Workers feel that the work they do is important. Note how the sentence about Chuck Long states that he is a great shipping clerk. After such a statement listeners know that you have respect for Chuck and the way he does his job. Say, "Any kid in the eighth grade could handle that job better," and you downrate yourself. Boost the characters you bring into a talk and listeners will like you better. One of my students asked me, "Supposing I tell a story about a panhandler; how can I boost him?" I heard a speaker do it thus, "This panhandler works on the corner by our office building. They tell me a Cadillac driven by a chaufeur in uniform comes to pick him up promptly at 4 p.m. every day." Mighty few listeners have a Cadillac driven by a chaufeur.

3. *Show Your Character Is Accepted:* Mention that Chuck, the shipping clerk, is on your bowling team and you show you think he is one of you. State that your boss is captain of the team, never misses a night and you show that the office is one happy family. State that you eat lunch with the boys from shipping or share a ride with them and you show that you are the right kind. How can you help yourself by telling that you eat lunch in the executive dining room.

4. *Boost Others' Accomplishments:* Every worker wants to feel that he is good at his job. The remarks about Chuck Long show how to do that. If you don't understand why the advertising department of your company is using a theme, don't say,

"Some knucklehead produced it." Such a line may get a laugh, but it indicates that you are smarter than somebody. Say something like, "These fellows in advertising have always come up with winners. How do we know this one we don't like isn't a winner?" Listeners can't assume that you know more about any subject than the ones who are paid to handle it. Any depreciatory opinion on subjects out of your field can picture you as a know it all. Boost the other work or don't talk about it.

5. *Compliment the Characters:* The advice so far on handling people suggests that you use the compliment generously. The sports hero shows how to do this. The hero says, "Give the other members of the team the credit. They did their jobs well and that allowed me to do my thing." Use this "member-of-the-team" idea when you talk about people. It helps in business, at the club and in social contacts. When the membership chairman of a club was complimented on the success of a drive, he said, "The members did it, no member brought in more than one application, and we got 86 new members. Figure it out—that meant a great number were working. Right? They deserve the credit." This type of statement shows the speaker is no credit grabber. Any compliment you pay a character makes you look better.

6. *Reveal How You Ask for Advice:* Tell you asked the mechanic who came to fix the air conditioner, "Got any idea where I could buy a good used two-wheeler bicycle?" What does such a question show your listeners? That you recognized the air conditioning man as a human being with the same problems you have. Treat all characters this way. You may be a big shot but you figured the smaller one might have some ideas, and so you asked. Now report what he told you and how you followed his advice. I heard a secretary tell about how she went down to the company garage and asked a mechanic about a funny noise in her car engine. She said, "You know how a mechanic thinks about a female's knowledge of anything mechanical. Well, I got an explanation in A.B.Cs." Be the one who doesn't hesitate to ask for advice or directions. The knack builds acceptance with your audience.

7. *Show You Listen to Others:* Most little people complain, "Nobody listens to me." Let your accounts show you are not among those nobodies. When a character in your story says something, ask him, "Is this what you mean?" He'll reply, "You got it right, Mister." Such an exchange shows you are not too important to listen to others. A report on your listening gives the audience the impression that you are a good guy. You listen. You lose face when you make a statement like, "I've got no time to listen to that kind of nut."

I have a line that gets a great laugh for me. I tell a story about meeting a drunk on the street who starts a conversation with me. I say, "But, ladies and gentlemen, this was ten o'clock in the morning and when I meet a character who is already stewed to the gills at ten o'clock in the morning, I have met a genius, and I've got time to stop to talk to him."

Picture yourself as a listener and you'll make friends. Remember you learned most of what you know by listening.

PEOPLE ARE MOST INTERESTED IN PEOPLE

Your newspaper this evening will have about 14 headlines on the front page. All but two or three of those headlines will mention people. People are mentioned in those headlines because the editors know that readers like to read about people. A headline, "Man Beats Up Wife" will get ten times the attention as one that mentions some ruling of the F.T.C. Use this idea in your speeches—

Put people in your information; tell about the fellow who dug up the data and how much work it took to get it. There is a chance for eloquence here. Say something like, "I went to Jane Getty and asked her how much work it would be to get this data. Now Jane's got enough work for three people without taking on more work for me, but she didn't hesitate, she said she'd get it, and she did. That's the spirit of the people we got working with us."

Have characters give your evidence. Here's what Tom Pinson found out, and May Wallace and Karen Worthy.

Quote them. Report their answers to your audience.

Make people a part of your talk and you are easier to listen to. Of course, you will put people in your stories, but think of putting them into your other data. Characters can help brighten any idea you plan to express.

THE CHARACTER ANGLE HAS PULL

Let's analyze the story about the plant closing mentioned in Chapter 15.

Ok, a factory closed. The listener can say, "Factories are closing every day."

120 jobs eliminated. That follows, there are other jobs.

Over 500 men, women and children with no income coming in. This is tragic in a land of plenty. What can the listeners do?

Now report what the dislocated say, the men, the wives, the children. The listener feels for every one of them.

Note how the interest builds up. The statement about the factory closing has some interest, as does the 120 jobs, but when the talk brings in the affected people, the listeners want to know more.

Use the statistics, but bring on what these statistics mean to people. Talk about such tragedies as the family refused credit at the grocery store, the store owner giving up a business that he had spent a lifetime building, the proud man commiting suicide before he would apply for relief. The human results have power. Use them and you will build up interest.

WATCH HOW YOU HANDLE YOUR MOST IMPORTANT CHARACTER–YOU

Finally, watch how you handle that most important person—*you.* Let this character laugh at the right things, cry with those who need sympathy. Make him one who fits into the group. This may be difficult, but give your speaker any breaks you can.

When using humor, let it be rough on you, but easy on the other fellow. When handling eloquence, let it involve you deeply. Show your concern, commitment, enthusiasm, by the feelings you display. Have the characters that give testimony show these same feelings.

PUT PEOPLE IN YOUR APPEALS, IN YOUR HUMOR

The banana peel on the sidewalk isn't funny, but when the fat tycoon slips on it you laugh. Your cause is empty without an appreciation of the people it benefits. Let the characters you know help you in your speeches. They bring life and reality to any speaking effort.

17

CONVERSATION ADDS ITS TOUCH

Two individuals are talking in an elevator as you get on. You don't know them, you don't know what they are talking about, you don't know the people they mention, but you try to listen. Eavesdropping–no–you are doing what comes naturally. Successful speakers use this desire to listen to build up any mood they want–perhaps humor, maybe eloquence.

HOW CONVERSATION MAKES FOR HUMOR

Supposing you say, "Sunday I was walking across the church parking lot and saw this fellow sitting in his car reading a paper. I glanced at the paper and saw it was a green racing form."

That's an interesting bit for the listeners. You make it better when you ask, "What are you going to do, Andy, pray for a horse?"

Your question could start an interesting exchange for everybody is asking, "What did he say?" You might say nothing in the parking lot and then be mightily surprised in church when you saw this same fellow passing the collection plate. You'd make that bit more interesting if later you reported, you asked him, "What do you think those people thought, Andy, when they saw you passing the collection plate with that racing form sticking out of your pocket?"

Now what he said and what you said takes on the nature of humor. It might be your explanation of why you were wearing a black eye home from church.

A SLIGHT SWITCH AND YOU VEER TOWARD ELOQUENCE

Supposing when you started the conversation, Andy said, "It's my weakness, Sam. I'm a compulsive gambler."

Now you report what he tells you—

He keeps himself constantly in debt.

His kids wear worn shoes because he gambles away his money.

His marriage is on the rocks.

His clothes are worn and threadbare.

He has tried and tried to stop.

The doctors work with him, but they tell him there is no hope.

With even a portion of this you have surely induced some of your listeners to think about looking up the telephone number of "Gamblers Anonymous."

This shows how the contact with the horse-player in the church parking lot can be slanted at humor or eloquence. The conversation, what you say and what the other says can make it anything you want.

CONVERSATION ADDS LIFE

Let the characters in your speeches speak and you can add humor or eloquence to what you say. Their answers arguing with you, testifying for you or giving you information bring in another party. You were alone, now there are two of you. It is easier to listen to two speakers. Look at a printed page and you see how a few lines of conversation make it look easier to read.

The same is true of the conversation you introduce in a speech. It is livelier than description, reason why, or other material. Note how the TV commercials use conversation. They know straight talk is good, but conversation can do it better. The man in the butcher shop tells the lady how to cook a chicken with the sponsor's product. She asks questions, he answers. You don't have any chickens to fry, but you listen to his story. Report in your speech that you told the bus driver, "Go easy on that brake today, Butch." Listeners ask, "And what did he say?" They sense it was probably a mouthful. And that mouthful can be mighty interesting. They know what they'd say if some joker told them how to drive a bus. If that mouthful helps prove the point you are trying to make, it has plus values. It holds interest, offers testimony, and introduces humor or emotion.

You might ask, "What kind of point can you make with a silly remark like that?" Let's say your subject is "We Make Most of Our Troubles with Our Big Mouths." Ok, here's a time you opened your big mouth when you should have kept it shut and the listeners think any lambasting you get from Butch serves you right. I got this bus driver incident from a woman speaker. She told what the driver said and concluded, "No self-respecting bus driver is going to let a female tell him how to drive a bus." Her theme was that what we say gets us into trouble.

THERE IS HUMOR IN CONVERSATION

Most funny stories depend for the laugh on something somebody says. The laugh comes because the remark is unexpected, it is ridiculous, or it is so right. It might show up the smart aleck, the wise guy or the big shot for what he is. But the humor comes with that last remark the character makes. There is a suggestion of humor in the man sitting in his car in the church parking lot reading the racing form as he waited for the church service. This is built up with the further news that the character passed the collection plate. The listeners enjoy the thought of such a situation. But the big laugh comes with the last remark of the racing form student. Just examine these situations—

In the Unexpected: You report that you went into the boss's office and said, "I'd like to talk to you about this idea of mine."

He answers, "How'd you like a slap in the puss?"

You ask, "You drunk?"

He says, "No, but I'm about to get disorderly if you don't get the hell outa here."

This is wholly unreal, wholly unexpected. Listeners look at you wondering what kind of boss you work for. You look baffled too. They suspect this must be some sort of gag but they wonder as they wait for your explanation.

In the Ridiculous: In one of my speeches I tell a story about a young man calling on a girl for the first time. She isn't ready when he arrives and he is asked to take a seat in the living room. While he waits the girl's mother, a giant of a woman he had never met, descends on him and asks, "What are your intentions toward my daughter?"

The point I am making in the speech is that by asking questions you can get out of any difficulty. The young man had been taught this procedure, but the question he thought of was, "How far will she go?"

That is a ridiculous question and it gets quite a laugh.

The point, "You do better if you ask the right questions."

Any story about animals that talk uses the ridiculous. You say, "This kangaroo went into a bar and ordered a double martini extra dry." The listeners get ready for a laugh, because this is an unbelievable situation.

In Big Words: Impressive words can be used to get laughs. Here is a statement by a professor whose wife had asked for an expensive bracelet she had seen in a jewelry store window.

"My, dear, inexplicable circumstances perforce preclude the eventuality of my endowing you with such an estimable bauble."

She said, "I don't get it."

He answered, "Precisely."

The use of these impressive words by characters who might not be expected to use them also is humorous. For instance one sailor said, "The food on our ship is good." His buddy said, "It is not, it's redundant and monotonous."

In the "So Right": The Sunday School teacher asks her small fry, "How many angels can sit on the head of a pin?" She looks for a response and after a wait one young man holds up his hand. "You have the answer, Johnny?" she asks. "What is your idea?"

"More than can sit on the point."

Let's say you report the top executive of your company started sending inspirational letters at intervals to the employees of your company. After a few of the letters had gone out, he decided to interview some of the employees to find out what they thought of them. He asked John Carew, "Do you get those letters I send out?"

John said, "Yes."

"Do you read them?"

"Yes."

"What do you think of them?"

"Ok, I figured we needed more stuff to fill the waste baskets."

Every listener knows of cases where his superiors have been cut down to size in this way and so he enjoys the bit of conversation.

In the Come Uppance: At the office you run onto two of your assistants arguing about a bit of work. You ask, "What's the trouble?" One says, "Keep your big nose outa this." The other adds, "Yeah, get lost." Ok, maybe you are the boss, but this exchange doesn't sound too much as if you are in control. The listeners are pleased because they figured you butted into something you should have let lie. A line or two of conversation can show a big shot being cut down to size and most groups, even big shots, laugh at the thought. Who understands such situations better than a big shot?

CONVERSATION ALSO HELPS IN ELOQUENCE

Words play a great part in any eloquence you attempt. Quote the words of the national hero, "Give me liberty or give me death." Quote what Mr. Lincoln said to the man who berated him for not putting him on the Federal payroll. These words were said by men. You asked the great man, "Why do you stand out above others?" He answered, "Maybe I work a bit harder." Ask him to elaborate and his answers give you the foundation of an eloquent bit. You feel your group is goofing off on production. His answers on, "Maybe I work a bit harder" can be bent right to your theme. Use the words of a young man, crippled for life, using a wheelchair to get around. He answered your first question, you asked him to say more, he said it, and what you report can inspire others not so handicapped. Ideas, ideals, thoughts, fundamental truths are the basis of most eloquence. With conversation you can repeat them, emphasize them in an interesting way by telling what others say about them.

HOW TO USE CONVERSATION

1. *Make It Sound Natural:* Many times when you hear a TV commercial you think, "That user would never have said, 'It's an exclusive feature.' She probably would have said, 'No other product has it!'" Last night I heard a speaker report, "He said something I didn't believe and was he right?" That "was he right" sounds as if someone spoke the words. One way to achieve naturalness is to use contractions. Don't report the character said, "He was not here." Make that, "He wasn't here." Not, "She cannot." Make it, "She can't." Can't you see the character who says, "He's got a crust."

2. *Keep It in Character:* If the characters might use slang, use it. Let your character say,

"Better if I stood in bed," or,

"No dice," or,

"It's a cloud of horsefeathers," or,

"How come you didn't send me a birthday card?"

This is how people talk and your information or testimony backed up by conversation that sounds real helps the listener believe. Watch big words that your character might never use unless you are trying for humor by giving him the big word to say.

3. *Keep Up to Date:* In the old melodrama, the hero ordered the villian, "Unhand that maiden." In today's language that

would be, "Take your cotton-pickin' hands off that dame." Try for conversation of the kind the listener hears every day.

4. *Forget Long Speeches:* Stick to short speeches by your characters. The long statement is difficult to follow. Note this the next time you hear an individual interviewed on TV. The interviewer puts so many words in the question that the one interviewed should ask, "Will you please repeat the question?" The interviewer couldn't possibly. Keep each speech down to ten words or less. One character says ten words, the second character answers in ten words or less. Don't allow either of them to talk on and on. Short exchanges give variety and speed the action.

5. *Use Strong Language When It Fits:* This is particularly true in eloquence. When you quote that third party let him speak with fire. No pussyfooting or equivocating. Let, him say, "This is no damned good." That's what was said, isn't it? Put as much force into what was said as the speaker did. When asked in the U.N. how long he would wait, Adlai Stevenson answered, " 'til Hell freezes over." You don't think he whispered those words, do you? Tell the audience you were threatened and the listeners ask, "With what?" Say, "The bully said, "I'll tear you in two and pound the halves down into the ground." Which gives a better picture of your opponent?

6. *Speak Slowly and Distinctly:* This advice applies to all speech, but it applies particularly to conversation. The listener wants to hear what the character said. If the remark isn't heard your point is lost. This is demonstrated for you on TV when the speaker rushes what he said. Your spouse laughed, but not you. You didn't hear. Slowing up has been mentioned before and is mentioned again to emphasize its importance with certain lines. Both sides of a conversation must be heard to be understood. Answers or retorts mean little if you don't hear the question or remark that brought them on.

7. *Help the Listener Understand Who Is Speaking:* Change your voice a bit or use the pause between speeches to indicate who is speaking. This speeds up the story. You won't need to say, "Tom said" and "Bill answered" except to indicate who is in the conversation.

HOW TO MANUFACTURE CONVERSATION TO STRENGTHEN YOUR POINT

One of the men in my speech clinic asked, "You mean we should manufacture conversation?" It is not difficult. Change a few words in a conversation and you can make any point you want. You ask a worker for his opinion of your product. He says, "Purty good." You want him to say, "Best I ever used." So you ask another question, "Would you say it is as good as any you ever used?" "Yes, I could say that." Now your third question, "Would you say it is the best you ever used?" He says, "I honestly believe that it is the best." Now you got what you want. In using the bit in a speech, you might use only his last remark. Or you might use all three questions and his replies. But the example shows how you can work over conversation to make it more helpful to you.

PEOPLE COME ALIVE WHEN THEY TALK

Somewhere I read, "Dialogue is thought in action." Doesn't each remark that follows give you a picture of the kind of person that made it? (These are story lines quoted in this book)

> "How'd you like a slap in the puss?"
>
> "How far will she go?"
>
> "It's redundant and monotonous."
>
> "Keep your big nose outa this."
>
> "Yeah, get lost."
>
> "He's got a lot of crust."
>
> "Take your cotton-pickin' hands off that dame."

By using the words in the way your characters would use them you explain something about the kind of people speaking. The words help, the feeling add power. A character's words can make the person sound stuffy, high-hat, uneducated, belligerant, chicken or whatever you will. Listeners know most of these types and your story sounds more authentic when your characters sound like real people living in a today's world.

Every one of those lines I repeated must be said with feeling. Try saying–

"Get lost."

Without showing any feeling. You can't. And if you report that another said the words, you'll say them with about the strong feeling your character put into them.

THE LISTENER WANTS TO HEAR–TELL HIM

You tell Chuck,

"I told my wife she better change butchers."

Chuck asks,

"What did she say?"

This is the usual pattern. The listener wants to know what the other said.

The gag line in a story is usually a bit of conversation. Think of what the doorman said when the guest told him to take care of his expensive car, "I got one exactly like it, but mine's got white side walls."

Any testimony that arouses emotion is a bit of conversation. The boy gave all his money to the small boy he thought underprivileged. You asked why and he said, "He needed it more than me." That bit of conversation could arouse a bit of emotion in every listener.

You can produce either humor or eloquence by reporting what both said. The listeners are asking. "What did she say?" Give them what they want.

18

THERE ARE LAUGHS, CHEERS OR TEARS IN NEWS

Think of your sources of news—

the newspapers
the radio and TV
the magazine
your daily contacts bring news in gossip form
your wife tells you that Angie is divorcing Tim
your son tells you about the fight at school
someone at the office passes you a rumor.

Every hour of every day you are exposed to items of fact or fiction in the guise of news. Because you and your listeners are living in the center of this avalanche, news makes good speech material. Your handling can shape it for humor or eloquence.

LISTENERS LOVE TO LISTEN TO NEWS

Think of the news sources I mentioned. How much time do you spend each day reading or listening? Ten minutes, thirty, an hour or more? You are not alone in this. I know a glutton who reads every article in *Time* and *Newsweek* each week, his daily newpaper and *Wall Street Journal.* Then, too, he listens to the radio and TV. You surely don't equal his record, but you are exposed to enough news to make your speeches easier to listen to if you will use the news items.

STOP WAITING FOR BIG NEWS

When I speak of news, I don't refer to items that are big enough to make the front page of your newspapers. Today if you made a note of everything that happened to you, or what you did, thought or said, you'd have quite a volume of speech material. This is the type of thing I mean–

Let's say you are working on a speech with the tentative title, *Nothing Is So Permanent as Change.* As you start to make notes you look up and see Johnny Martin, one of the bright young men in accounts receivable, walking through the outer office passing out cigars. "Here's a bit of news you say. The Martins have a new baby." When he reaches you, you say, "Congratulations–What is it, Johnny, he or she?"

"A boy," he replies.

"Johnny Martin, Junior?" you ask.

"How'd you guess?"

Thinking of your speech on change, you ask, "This make any change in your living plans?"

"Yes, it does. I haven't made a list yet, but we'll have to get out of the apartment, not enough room."

"Anything else?"

"I'll have to get more life insurance, I guess."

You can carry these analysis questions to any length. Your news–the Martins have a baby. It means change for the Martins, just as it does for the millions of other new parents who had additions to the family that week. Increase in population is one of the causes of change. The listener relates to such talk because he remembers, "Yeah, that's how it was with us when Gregory was born."

You might ask, "What kind of listeners will be interested in Johnny Martin's baby?"

Almost everybody. I guarantee that. And look at how easily the news came to you. While others might wait for some item of greater importance, you took what dropped into your lap and fashioned a news story that would help you make your point in a speech. If you have some angle on a larger news item, like a flood or earthquake that will help prove your point, use that. But don't wait for it. This morning the little girl on the bus slapped the big guy. "You can't pinch me, you big gorilla," she cried. That is a small bit of news perhaps, but audiences will listen to it because it is perhaps as big as any news they came across this week.

SMALL NEWS COMES TO YOU

Once or twice in our lives a big item of news will drop into our laps, but the small items come every day. Think of these possibilities–

Your wife goes on a diet

Your son wins a trip to Europe

The little old lady pushes ahead of the big lug in the cafeteria line. The big lug lifts her bodily and puts her back where she belongs.

These things happen every day, and they make good speech material.

HOW TO USE SUCH NEWS FOR HUMOR OR ELOQUENCE

Your wife on a diet suggests comedy. But suppose she asks the family to diet with her. Now the menus are too light for you and the children. Couldn't you get eloquent on that theme? Starving her family to lose a few pounds off her hips.

Your boy won the trip to Europe, not because he wanted to go, but because he wanted to keep another boy from winning it. So he worked day and night on his project. There is eloquence possibilities in your account of how he worked, did research at the library, wrote and rewrote his paper. You protested that he was working too hard, that a trip to Europe wasn't worth endangering his health. He agreed, said, "I know that. I don't want to go to Europe at all." "Then why are you putting yourself to all of this bother?" you ask. He says, "To keep Jackson from getting the trip." I heard this story used in a talk called, "The Evils of Competition." You might go on and tell how your son felt so badly about taking the trip away from the other boy that he moped about for three or four days. You suspected what was bothering him. He had told you that the other boy wanted so much to make the trip to visit grandparents over there. The next you heard, your son had arranged to have the trip transferred to the other boy. Can't you express some feeling about the act. You are proud of him for doing it, right?

A SLIGHT CHANGE AND YOU HAVE HUMOR

Suppose the end of your story was what the boy said when you congratulated him on winning. "Thanks, Mom but now I'm stuck with a trip to Europe." The incident of the little old lady and the big lug could be either humor or eloquence, the big lug watched her push ahead of a line of people, then he went up to get her. He picked her up, carried her back to where she belonged and said, "I've told you not to push ahead of people like that, Mother." For eloquence make either of them a disliked character, him because of his size, she because of her peskiness and disregard of others. Your imagination can take on from there, I'm sure.

INDUCE QUESTIONS AND YOU ADD INTEREST

Any of the news items mentioned will bring questions from listeners.

Mention your wife's diet and they ask, "What kind of diet?"

Tell about the contest and they ask, "What did your boy have to do to win the trip?"

That's why news is good. Listeners want to know more.

I tell you Joe got himself engaged over the weekend.

Joe is my friend and your friend. Ok, how many questions can you think to ask?

A speaker explains how rumors can cause trouble by citing his own experience. He was the principal character in a rumor that had him being transferred to Philadelphia to head up the company's operations there. A fine promotion, that he first heard of when one of his associates came into his office, closed the door, and congratulated him on the move. He protested that he knew nothing, but he got no place with his denial. The fellow said, "I guess you were told not to say anything yet, huh?" The informant left with, "It couldn't happen to a nicer guy. Remember, I said that." Next his wife came into the office, something she seldom did. He could tell she was disturbed. Her beef was, "Why did you agree to go to Philadelphia without consulting me. We're a partnership, right?" He protested he knew nothing. She said, "You know you can't lie to me. I can always tell." That evening his teenage daughter issued an ultimatum, "I'll leave this family if we have to move to Philadelphia."

In less than two minutes of speaking he got himself into a predicament because of a rumor that somebody had started. This is good speech technique—the listeners can see him, they can imagine him in the dark, afraid to ask, afraid not to ask, just as they can imagine themselves in the midst of such confusion. The boys at the office, the spouse and kids are all real to them. He said his wife was disturbed, maybe a listener would describe his wife as being madder than a wet hen. But the speaker was welcomed to their club. His problems paralleled theirs.

HOW TO MAKE NEWS ITEMS IMPORTANT TO THE LISTENER

Here are some ideas:

1. *Slant at Your Point:* Work over each item you use so that it offers the evidence to help prove your point. Perhaps a bit of changing here and there can help. You saw the little girl on the bus slap the big guy. In your speech you picture yourself as the guy that was slapped. To make your point you say she slapped you and called you "a big gorilla." You explain that you were reading your newspaper and hadn't noticed the girl. The listeners are inclined to believe you, you are not big, you don't resemble a gorilla, and you don't seem like the kind of fellow

that would pinch a girl on a bus. They suspect you brought up this item as a bit of humor. If your objective is a laugh you have them in the mood for it. Now go on, tell about your argument with the bus driver, the cop, and perhaps one or more of the passengers. If your point was that a citizen going about his business can find himself in trouble, the shift of characters has helped you emphasize your point. If you had not changed the story, listeners might say, "Maybe the big gorilla did pinch the poor girl." A change such as the one illustrated may be needed in many of your "for instances." You are trying to make a point. Changing your characters, what they say, or what they do helps accomplish your objectives.

2. *Tell Why Your News Is Important:* Johnny Martin's change in the size of his family was important to him, but why is it important to the listeners? Give some reasons why. Johnny is only one case, but there are thousands like Johnny–think of the large market these changes open up–cite the increase in spending Johnny faces multiplied by the number of births in the city, county or state. Tell them, "This is important to us because–" For instance, at lunch the waitress spilled a bowl of soup over your left shoulder and all over the front of your coat. That might call for a laugh until you explained you had a date that afternoon to present a most important plan to the management committee of your company. Thirty minutes before your big opportunity, the accident stripped you to your shirt sleeves. The soup on the coat was an accident, having it happen just minutes before your big chance made it a small tragedy. Note that each happening is news to the audience.

3. *Act as if It Is Important:* When you are using a news item to make a point for the plan you want the club to adopt, treat it seriously. You can't win recruits for your plan by joking about it. The rumor that you are being transferred to Philadelphia is not too important. But when your wife takes the attitude she does, and your daughter rebels, you got problems thrust upon you. Show your attitude about those problems. Act as if you'd like to clobber those rumor mongers. Your words and your attitude strengthen your point that rumors waste too much time.

4. *Talk Excitedly About It:* If you are presenting a new plan to your group, show by the way you talk that you are sold on it. It is good, it is better, it is the best. Let your enthusiasm boil over. Don't present your data and assume that facts will do the job for you. If your survey showed 82% of the membership wanted this plan, state that fact. Then emphasize the fact, "Think of that, eight out of ten of the members want this." Remember some of any enthusiasm you show rubs off on your audience.

5. *Give Any Plan or Product News Value:* When you are presenting a plan or a product, mention what's new about it. Then tell what these new benefits mean to the listeners. Tell why the changes were made, what the changes will do to help users or members. In the TV commercials the auto maker says that his new welded body is built like a space ship. Most listeners are asking, "What's new about that?" Tell them and you will add interest.

6. *Show Anything Printed:* If the news item is out of a newspaper or magazine, show it. Listeners place great belief in what they see in print. Chapter 21 gives many suggestions for visuals.

BUILD UP YOUR NEWS WITH THESE DEVICES

Tell a story about it.
Put people in it, and
Use conversation to make it more interesting.

These devices rate as good speech material and all can be used to make your news more interesting.

NEWS IS EASY TO FIND, EASY TO LISTEN TO

Think of news as something you know that I don't, or that I know and you don't. I mention Chuck's wife. You say, "I didn't know he had a wife." That was news to you. Don't think of news only as the big stories that call for the large black type on the front page of the newspaper. You won't find too many of that kind. But Dagwood's remarks and antics are available every day. Small items can help you one day for humor, another for eloquence. And they come to you without any extra time spent in research.

19

YOUR POSSESSIONS GIVE YOU A GOLDMINE OF MATERIAL

The world is filled with common things.

A button pops off your coat. It rolls down the grating on the sidewalk.

That button is of prime interest to you. It has no interest to your neighbor. But neighbors will listen as you talk about it just as they would try to help you get it out from under that grating. Think of the possibilities. You tried to get your spouse to sew it on, you tried to get your teenage daughter to sew it on, you tried to sew it on yourself. That button is flooded with possibilities. Let's say you were out of town when it popped off, you went into three stores and tried to get three sales clerks interested in helping you find a button to match the ones on the coat. Indifference, exasperation, frustration.

Why will others listen to such small stuff? Well, that's a type of problem they understand. They laugh at your failures to get that button replaced. This is reality, such things have happened to them. Think of the points you can make with such accounts. The indifference of sales people to your problem, your standing at home—ok, you can think of others, can't you?

YOU HAVE THOUSANDS OF SUBJECTS

Some speakers may not think this kind of material is important enough to include in their offerings. But successful speakers use it. Listeners like it—talk about the shoestring that broke and you don't seem to be trying to overpower them with big ideas, logic, theory or knowledge. Shoestrings—they know.

HOW YOUR POSSESSIONS HELP

You Know Them Well, Listener Knows Them Well: The listener will understand about any problem you have with ordinary things. You wanted to wear a particlar blue shirt tonight, you had it all planned. When you looked for it, you remembered it was at the laundry. For a bit of humor you might have your wife tell you that your teen-age son had worn it. You ask, "Why did he have to take my best shirt, to go out with the same kids that see him every day looking like a rag picker?"

She defends him, "You are always telling him that he should dress up like you do."

This is the kind of problem you and your listeners share. Because you have problems they understand they relate to you.

You Show You Are like the Listeners: Remember how the little girl sang about her Alice Blue Gown? We all have memories of our prized possessions. Maybe you recall that beat-up jackknife your grandfather gave you when you were ten. Most kids had jackknives, most of them loved them. Think how eloquent you could get as you described your feelings when you discovered you had lost that knife. Your interest in such small things gives the impression that you are like—the people at the near desks at the office, those who buy football pool cards every week, ones who say what you do at petty exasperations. You are one of them and you rate high.

Listeners Measure You for Size: Mention your Cadillac if it helps you make a point, but don't make it a brand-new Caddy, please? Most listeners will be driving smaller cars, and ones with miles and miles on them. Mention that you bought the Caddy off a used car lot—you believe in living dangerously. The man had it priced so low that the first check you wanted to make was to look under the hood and see if it had an engine. In using any possession try to make it the kind that any of the group would own and understand.

You Have Such a Variety: Think of the adventures and misadventures you have with the simple articles you own, work or play with. The blue and the pink pills the doctor gave you, you're supposed to take a pink one every two hours and a blue one every four hours, or is it the reverse, the blue every two, and the pink every four? Your small son leaves his roller skates on the basement steps. Your neighbor who borrowed your book that made the best-seller list. Now you can't brag that you have read it because you don't have it to lend. Think of points such adventures will help you make. In one of my sessions I mentioned a necktie as a good subject. One man said, "Some guys don't wear neckties."

Another put in, "Then talk about Adams apples."

A third asked, "Which is purtier, a necktie or an Adams apple."

It comes out speech material either way.

HOW TO USE SUCH POSSESSIONS TO MAKE POINTS

The introduction of neckties and Adam's apples helps in speech making because they can make points. Check through these examples of how to use possessions you and listeners live with every day. Note how I've heard them used for humor or for eloquence.

1. *Your Car:* Any listener in your audience thinks of his car as one of the most interesting things in his life. You had a rattle in the trunk, you took it to the service station, the boys looked for it, charged you eight bucks, but nothing was changed. The rattle was still there laughing at you. You wrote to the nice guy from the manufacturer you saw on TV who asked you to write. Now you tell about the prompt service or the run around you

got. You can bet your listeners would be interested. They have wondered what would happen if they wrote or telephoned that nice guy so willing and eager to help you. Talk about your car is better if you are driving a beat up jalopy while your teenager uses the family car to get back and forth from high school. Suppose your car were stolen. Couldn't you get eloquent describing your feelings when you first realized that your car was gone. Your listener can relate to such a situation. But any adventure with the car is interesting because that car is so much a part of our daily lives.

2. *Your Purchases:* Accounts of your adventures in retail stores make interesting material. The salesman tells you that the hat you are trying on does something for you. The way he says that "something" indicates that it gives you a flair, perhaps a dash of youth. You look again in the mirror and you think, perhaps, you can see what he means. It does do something for you. You figured on paying ten bucks for a hat, and this one with the flair is twenty-two. You confide to the group. "At my age acquiring that flair comes more expensive." You came out of the liquor store carrying two brown bags, each loaded with bottles of bourbon and ran into two gossipy old ladies from your church. The ladies spoke with a knowing smile and went on down the row and into another store. You got into your car and sat there for a while. In a few minutes you saw the old ladies on the sidewalk again. They looked about, and then went into the liquor store. You explain you didn't wait until they came out to see what they bought, for that would be spying. Let's say you bought a toy for a youngster for his birthday. The toy was easy to put together, the package said. You took it to the youngster and showed him the picture on the package. Then you tried to follow the instructions. The description of your frustration and anguish should furnish both eloquence, or humor.

3. *Your Office:* The office manager asked you if you would like one of the big oriental rugs they were taking out of the top executive's offices. You agreed to take one. When you arrived the next morning you saw that the jokers who put down the rug

had put the worn place in front of the door where it could be seen. You asked the office manager to have the men back to turn the rug so that the worn place would be in the other corner behind the desk and under the bookcase and the waste basket. He said that the budget for that work was all spent. "Besides, you shouldn't look a gift horse in the mouth," he added. A mix-up like this is common to most offices and the listeners can appreciate your predicament. The boss makes a rule that all papers are to be put together with clips. You prefer staples, but the boss tore his finger on a staple. As you read about such office confusion, you think of things that happen at your office. They can make good speech material. All offices are different, but all have mishaps and successes that others will listen to with interest. Small talk, maybe, but our lives are filled with that kind of small talk. There is humor in it, and eloquence too.

4. *Your Projects:* Your garden is good. I heard a member tell a garden club about her green thumb. When she first started she was tremendously proud of the riot of color she achieved with her petunias. Then a neighbor showed her a magazine article which quoted an old saying, "Any idiot can grow petunias." There is comedy in that. But let's assume the neighbor's cat has a habit of running through your garden and knocking over the small delphinium plants. One has been broken off three times this spring, but each time you sprinkled a bit of root powder on the broken end, replanted it, and each time it has grown new roots and is growing well now. That's an idea for an eloquent bit on persistence. When we are knocked over, do we get up and try again? Relate how you built this peg board and got your tools arranged so neatly on it. When you took your brother-in-law to see it, the kids had been using the tools and you spent maybe twenty minutes getting them back in their proper places. Talk about your golf game, your tennis, your daring to umpire the softball game for the kid's team. The racing car you helped Junior make for the Boy Scout pine knot derby. These are the kinds of things that your listeners experience. As you talk about them, you picture yourself as a likeable human being. And the accounts add evidence that helps build up points.

5. *Your Home:* Talk about any do-it-yourself job and you hold interest. You were lucky when you knocked over the gallon of paint. It spilled on the ground, well, not really the ground, it was your wife's garden. She was a bit unreasonable about it, you had to dig all the dirt out and replace it. You tell about the days when your wife wanted a crystal chandelier for your dining room. After listening to her story of what it would do for the room you agreed that maybe it would help. She selected one, and put it up. A week after the installation the fat-ladies bridge club came in for lunch. They ate under the new chandelier, and not one of them mentioned it. But Mommy had her crystal chandelier, and there was peace in the family until another want came along. Think of such examples in your home and use them. They will hold attention. And they can help you make points.

6. *Your Pets:* The animal world can help. Yesterday I saw a small red squirrel in a tree right outside my bedroom window. I stopped to look at him, he turned to look at me. He had a small pine cone in his mouth. I admired the color of his coat as winter approached. I once used the story of the cardinal that saw his reflection in one of my storm windows and flew at the reflection again and again. Each time the collision with the window knocked the bird to the frozen ground. For weeks he tried to drive away that rival. I used the incident to make the point that it helps to know what you are striving for. I talk about Puddles, a dog that lives with my grandchildren. He is one of these pups that jumps all over you when he sees you. He accepts me, but I have a difficult time accepting him. The common pets are best for such illustrations. I use an incident of my three year old grandson watching a spider weave a web and asking me, "Grandad where does that spider get that string he is using?" "From himself," is the answer. Think of the use of that thought in a bit of eloquence making the point–all improvement is self-improvement, it comes from within you.

7. *Your Clothes:* I showed how the button that popped off your overcoat could be used. At one time I did a talk, "How To Run A Meeting." One point was that the speaker dress well, for what listener wanted to take advice from an individual who

looked as if he slept in his clothes? I explained my preparation, dark blue suit, white shirt and a red tie. Years later, when I appeared on a program, a listener told me, "You haven't got on your red tie tonight." I'll bet that man didn't remember another point I made in that first talk. I've used a story about a millionaire boss I had and his attraction to gray suede shoes. He'd stand in front of the shoe-store window and say, "I wish I had enough money to afford a pair of shoes like that." What he really wished was that he had nerve enough to wear a pair of those shoes. (This was years ago.) Think of the possibilities of this story to help you make points with humor or eloquence. He could afford the suede shoes, he could have worn them, but he was held back by the fear of what people would say. It could point out how times have changed; today that man could have worn red suede shoes and nobody would have noticed. It could point out what our mental blocks do to us. The value of the shoes is that they can help you get a laugh, or arouse an emotion.

THE FORMULA FOR MAKING POSSESSIONS INTERESTING

Check back on these examples of how shoes, or ships or sealing wax can be used and find a pattern of use that includes these steps–

a. tell a story about the article.

b. put people in the story. You're in, have others join you.

c. talk to these people about the problem you are having with the thing.

Shakespeare said, "Sermons in stones." John Burroughs contradicted that with, "There are no sermons in stones." He did go on, "It is easier to get a spark out of a stone than a moral." Stones, shoestrings and collar buttons all make interesting speech material.

Listeners may laugh at the indifference of the sales people in helping you find a button that matched. They can also be incensed at that indifference. Your description of your frustration can arouse sympathy, anger or whatever emotion you want. Same incident, use one way and you get a laugh, use another way and you arouse emotion.

20

HOW TO EXTRACT HUMOR AND ELOQUENCE FROM FIGURES

Data–statistics–numbers.

Used properly they can help you be humorous or eloquent.

Statistics can help bring some of your laughs–the lady being congratulated on her 97th birthday said she never expects to die. Her basis for the thought, "Mighty few people over 97 years of age die." Statistics prove it.

Statistics can strengthen some of your emotional appeals. "Seven people living in an unheated room. That's poverty, squalor."

But to be good speech material figures take doctoring. Quote a few and the listeners might follow what you say. Load them on and attention flies out the window.

WHY LISTENERS DON'T LIKE FIGURES

Remember when you were in school most of the kids were poor at math. They were poor because they didn't like figures.

When you present your figures to listeners, they think back to those dreary math sessions. You may say, "Why I liked math." Fine, you and a few other kids may have liked the subject. But most of the class didn't. And as they grew older they didn't change. Even if your figures show the plain unvarnished truth, they will go over better with your audiences if you give them a bit of varnishing.

WHEN TO USE STATISTICS

Of course, there are times when you need figures to prove your point or to strengthen your case. At such times statistics can be most helpful. Here are some justifications:

When They Help Make Your Meaning Clear: Maybe you have a table of figures from the US Census to help make your meaning clear, but don't use it just because you have it. Use only as much of it as you feel necessary. If a few figures from the table will do the job, use the few. Remember with figures a good rule is the fewer the better. I asked one speaker why he discussed so many figures, "I did it to kill time," he said. He killed the time and he lost interest too.

When They Are Important: If your objective is to show that prices have gone up more than the public thinks, you need figures. You say, "Prices have gone up." You have agreement, for you see heads nodding. "But do you know how much?" To emphasize you bring on your specifies, you add, "Two months ago the product was eleven cents per bottle, today it is fourteen." What percentage increase is that? I figure about thirty. Thirty percent on the price of a car could cost you from five hundred to one thousand bucks."

The three cents per bottle might lead the listener to say, "It's only three cents." But that thirty percent gives another measure. When you think of using statistics, ask yourself this question, "Will it help me make, emphasize or clarify a point?" If you have any doubts, forget your numbers.

HOW TO MAKE FIGURES MORE PALATABLE

1. *Put in Story Form:* Tell a story about the figures. Tell the group, "I didn't believe it when I heard it, but I went down to the library and checked."

2. *Put People in Them:* You asked the girl in the library, who is an expert on this subject. She brought you four big books and explained how you could check the figures yourself.

3. *Report Some Conversation About Them:* You wrote down a number of figures from the books and took them back to the girl, you asked her if they meant this, she said, "Not quite that, but–" Conversation "what she said and what you said" will be listened to, and you can shape that conversation to emphasize your point.

4. *Mention Any News Value:* Say, "These figures are from the latest census and they haven't been released to the newspapers yet. The compilation was finished last night and you are the first to get the results," or "I got these out of this morning's newspaper." Make similar remarks and you arouse more interest in your figures.

5. *Keep Within the Listener's World:* Compare your figures with something the listeners know. A monsoon may mean little to them, but a hard rain that floods the lowlands may. Use the one they know. When you quote costs, compare with items they buy every day. Say, "A can of beer costs 50 cents in most bars." They know a can of beer.

6. *Personalize:* You say, "My car is ten years old, how old is yours?" Your story about car life now is a personal thing to him. The United Appeal wants $300,000.00. The listener asks, "How much does that mean from me?" You say, "It's easy to figure what to give, we ask for one day's pay. You know what you earn in one day. That's what makes a fair share gift." Figure out how to make your figure personal to them.

7. *Localize:* Say, "It's about twice as tall as the First Bank Building." The listeners see that building every day. Ask them to, "Go down to the Super-Market and check," and you are speaking their language. Explain, "It is about as far as from here to Seventh and Main." The local reference gives a clearer picture.

8. *Let the Listeners Help:* Ask them to guess the cost, to estimate how many. This brings them into a discussion of your figures and makes the figures come to life. Ask, "I'm not going to tell you this cost, you estimate it." This is like guessing the

number of pennies in the jar, and listeners will oblige. If you want them to shout out the answers, ask for that. Or after you have given them a few seconds to guess, give them the correct answer. Remember that everybody wants to get into the act. Chapter 23 gives many ideas on how to use audience participation.

9. *Use Visuals:* If you have one figure to emphasize, write it on a big card and hold it up for listeners to see. If you have more figures, use a chart or two. Chapter 21 offers ideas on the use of the many kinds of visuals available.

10. *Be Fair:* If you are using figures to persuade the group to do something, be fair. Claim too much and you lose followers who want to go along. Let's say your figure is 97% for your side, quote 62% and the listener will say, "It's more than that." But he is arguing on your side, not against you. Give the other side credit for being honest. If opponents have a good point, mention it and explain what you have to offset it. A visual showing the advantages and disadvantages of your plan can give the impression that you are trying to be fair.

11. *Don't Fake Any Figures:* Figures are supposed to represent facts, not fiction. If you can't find figures to substanstiate your premise, don't manufacture them. You'll know they are faked and you can't sound sincere using them. You know how you feel when you hear the toothpaste man say 28 percent less cavities. You ask, "How can he measure that?"

12. *Explain Any Figures That May Need Explanation:* At times you may quote a figure that needs explaining. Earlier in this chapter I mentioned the price increase for a bottle of soft drink from 11 to 14 cents. A speaker adds, "That's three cents a bottle." Most listeners might think that's not much. Then the speaker adds, "That's about thirty percent. Has your food money increased 30 percent?" If your figure sounds incredible to you, have a good explanation for it. If it sounds too good, and needs extra explanation, consider forgetting it.

13. *Cut the Detail:* Don't quote odd dollars over the millions, or odd cents over the dollars. Use even figures. You make the same impression by using seven million, as by using seven million one

hundred eleven thousand. The complete figure takes more time and concentration.

14. *Use as Few as Possible:* The fewer you use, the better the listeners like it. If you have figures for the past 25 years, there is no need to show each year. Show instead the changes for each five years.

15. *Don't Mention Beforehand:* You are not promising a treat when you say, "In a few minutes I'll show you some figures that will help prove my point." Bring on the good or sad news when you need it without fanfare. Why cause the listener to moan, "Oh, Lord, he's bringing on some statistics."

16. *Don't Apologize for Using:* I heard a speaker say, "I'm sorry that I have to bore you with these figures." Forget any such thought. If you have to use them, use them. A workman wouldn't apologize if he had to change to a sharper chisel. The figures are your tools, just as the chisel is his. If you need them, use them. Think of them as interesting and then do what you need to do to make them interesting.

FOLLOW THE SURE-FIRE FORMULA

If your figures are not too important, forget them. If they are important, doll them up–

tell stories about them
involve people
use conversation
compare with the commonplace
or use any of the 16 devices suggested.

FIGURES TALK, BUT HAVE FEW FRIENDS

Both Humor and Eloquence: I heard the speaker say, "It's a good restaurant, the food's good, but they give you too much. Order fried chicken and they bring you thirteen pieces." Such exaggeration is good for a smile. And how about that remark Uncle Slug made about the price you paid for a new suit? Without exaggeration you can stir a group by quoting figures of the amount of interest people in the ghetto were paying to get their homes repaired. Your concern for such injustice can rub off on listeners.

Start with the knowledge that listeners do not like statistics. Then go easy on them. Present your data in a way that makes it easier on your listeners. Put a bit of sugar on the bitter pill. It pays.

21

PICTURES HELP AROUSE EMOTIONS OR GET LAUGHS

A picture can help your appeal.

A picture can bring on a laugh.

On TV I saw a group of men and boys killing rats that infested their tenement. Some drove the rodents into the alleys, others finished them with heavy sticks.

A speaker could say, "This row of houses is infested with rats." He could go on, "Not a few rats, hundreds of them, yes, thousands." The words would give you some idea, but your feelings would not be as influenced as they could be by that picture.

Show a picture of a small child with its face scratched and bandaged. Let the listeners look, then ask, "What happened to this child's face?" Pause, then say, "Rats fed on it while she slept in her bed." Could you have a more eloquent appeal for cleaning up the slums?

LAUGHS INSTEAD OF TEARS

A visual can help you get a laugh. I heard the Comptroller of a giant company tell his audience, "The boys back at the office told me that this talk would be better with visuals. They told me listeners liked to look at visuals. Well, I didn't have time to make any visuals, and no budget to cover them, but I did do this. I got myself a visual–here it is." He unrolled a large calendar that showed a shapely young lady, generously endowed, yet scantily clad. He held up the picture for all to see. "I knew you'd like that," he went on. "I'll give you a minute to look at it, then I'll go on. But there will be no more visuals."

His visual got a laugh from some of his audience, a smile from others. There was humor in his handling of it, but the visual did not help him make his point or help in his story.

VISUALS CAN STAR IN A COMEDY SKETCH

You perhaps have seen a slide presentation designed to get laughs. The comedian sets up as if to do a serious speech and his assistant with the projector makes all kinds of mistakes, the wrong picture, the picture upside down, no picture just light. The comedian gets frustrated, he argues with the projector man. Personal insults fly back and forth. The speaker shouts, "You're fired." The projector man answers, "You can't fire me, I quit." The audience enjoys the spoof, the frustration, the argument. And the visuals carried much of the load.

SHOW GOOD SENSE BY USING VISUALS

You have heard the old Chinese proverb, "A picture is worth one thousand words." Most of our impressions come from what we see." Psychologists tell us that impressions come–

84% through the eyes,

9% through the ears, and

7% through other senses.

These figures give you an idea why the showing of a visual is important. It is why when the TV man wants you to write to his client, he shows you the name of the charity, the city and the p.o. box number. If you remember the city and the p.o. box number, you know where to write.

VISUALS HELP IN ELOQUENCE

I saw a missionary show a picture of a small boy carrying his little sister in a sling attached to his back. Both kids would arouse your sympathy. The caption had the small boy saying, "Would you support my little sister? She don't eat very much." The missionary was asking for contributions to support a whole home full of kids like these. He knew that his visual would pull at the heartstrings of listeners who would help feed those youngsters.

THE TYPES OF VISUALS USED BY SPEAKERS

Anything you show can be called a visual, a card out of your pocket, your wallet, a letter, a pencil all get attention. Here is a list of the types of visuals that speakers use—

Blackboard
Easel pad
Charts
Cards
Photographs
Cloth covered boards
Magnetic boards
Product or merchandise
Slides (rear projection or over the shoulder)
Film strips
Motion pictures (silent)

Some are inexpensive and are easy to obtain in most meeting locations, others are used when a talk is to be given a number of times. A consideration important to speakers is the difficulty of moving the visuals from one point to another. An easel pad can be rolled and carried easily. Some of the boards or projectors are bulkier. I list the different types of visuals to show what a wide variety the speaker has to choose from.

VISUALS GET THE LAUGH AND EMPHASIZE POINTS

In a management practices conference on handling employees, I saw a speaker show a cartoon of a sad sack in a box about the size of a small telephone booth. The sad sack was sitting on a stool, bent over, looking forlorn, dejected. The lettering under the picture said, "People Are No Damn Good." The picture got a laugh. Then the speaker explained, "I went into a manager's office the other day and saw this cartoon framed on the wall." I asked the manager, "Why do you have that picture on the wall?" He said, "It's the truth, isn't it?" The speaker then explained, "This man had over 60 employees reporting to him, and I asked him, 'If that's the truth, whose in trouble?' " The speaker didn't report the manager's answer, instead he brought in the listeners with a question to them, "Who is?"

The group answered, "The manager."

The cartoon was removed when it had served its purpose. But all day the conferees kept bringing it up. They would answer questions with, "I'm not a sad sack," or, "That's a sad-sack idea." It was an effective demonstration of how a visual can be used to emphasize a point.

DEMONSTRATE WHAT YOU CAN DO WITH A VISUAL

You have seen pictures of the starving refugees driven from their homes by war or disaster. Each face seems to be appealing to you for help. Let's assume you want to use such a picture to persuade your group to contribute to a fund to help feed these unfortunates. Try this thought I use in my speaking classes to show how eloquent any of us can be. I ask the student to study such a picture for two minutes and then tell the class why they should send two dollars to the Red Cross, already on the job helping the victims. The purpose of the drill is to show that each student can be eloquent after studying such a picture. The demonstration the speakers give is proof positive. They go all out describing the conditions of the sufferers. They demonstrate talent they didn't know they had.

TRY THIS IDEA AND SURPRISE YOURSELF

Try this yourself the next time you see a picture of a hungry child. Study the picture, figure out what you can say to an audience to ask for the contributions. You'll find strong words that appeal, you'll show your feelings and your talk will be eloquent. Try this with any subject about which you want to be eloquent. One student wrote me that a friend told him that he was living dangerously by mouthing so much criticism of his boss. "If you can't say something good about him, shut up," the friend ordered. "I thought of your eloquence stunt," he wrote, "I got a picture of the so and so, studied it, and asked myself what could I say good about him. I found plenty. How he had brought me along, listened to me, what I had learned from him, how he covered for me, stuff like that. Then I gave this pitch to the friend. 'I thought you hated his guts?' The friend laughed." Try this idea on any subject. You'll find that it makes an orator of you.

HOW THE VISUAL HELPS

Showing adds power to your persuasion. Maybe your words can tell the story, but you make it easier on the listener when you picture what you mean. Speakers know that "Listeners can stop listening, but they can't resist looking." Think how you benefit by showing something:

1. You Hold Attention Better

Many times when I tell trade association secretaries running a meeting that I have to set up a set of charts, they ask, "You travel with that set of charts?" They are surprised to hear that I feel the charts important enough to carry with me on planes. But I know that with my set of charts I am going to hold attention all through a talk. Show a new chart and every listener looks to see what is coming up. When a speaker shows a single chart the listener examines it to see what it is and what point the speaker is emphasizing with it. Assume that the meeting is being held in a room with a window that is opposite an office building across the street. A secretary moves in front of a window of the office building. Where does every eye go? Use a visual to compete with the girl in the window and you have a better chance in the competition.

2. You Bring Back Attention

A chart talk does this. If you note that listeners are beginning to tire, show another chart and attention comes back to what you show. I saw an instructor of public speaking take a small card out of his lapel pocket, hold it up, and ask, "Where is every eye in the room?" The listeners answered, "On the card." The listeners can't read what is printed on the small card, but they will look. For some reason listeners may not feel they lose anything when they stop listening to your words. But they want to see everything you show.

3. Visuals Allow You to Repeat

You tell the group that this latest boondoggle of the Government will cost every family $201. Some may not hear the figure, some may not understand. But when you show a card with "201 DOLLARS" on it, you give the listeners a second chance to understand. The successful speaker knows that even his best explanations may not explain too well, so he uses a visual that repeats to help clarify what he means. If the audience is taking notes, the visual helps the listener get the figure right.

4. They Give Relief

If the speaker is skilled in the use of visuals, he allows the visual to do the talking. Visuals help especially with figures. If my story says that there are just three figures that are important to us and then go on talking about the figures, I may lose you. But if I show you a chart with the three figures and say, "These are the three figures that are important," there is no need to talk about the figures–my visual shows them to you. A picture of the hungry children is much more interesting than my word description of those hungry children. The TV advertisers know that you would rather look than listen. They break up the talk with pictures. Watch how they do it and you'll get ideas on how to use their techniques in your speeches.

5. They Make the Story Easier to Follow:

A speaker could make a five minute talk on what always happens to dictators, but that picture of the great general and his horse knocked off the pedestal and lying in the rubble of the gutter is easier on the attention. The listener looks and says, "So true." You can speak for quite a time about the savings your plan would make, but the listener might say, "I can't see how it would save that much." Show a chart that lists those savings and he can see how you figured them. They help provide proof because we believe what we see in print.

6. They Help in Retention

The TV salesman who shows you the p.o. box number knows you have a better chance of remembering it than if he had told it to you. A speaker told a group, "I'm not going to talk a long time about the savings you can make on your auto insurance. I am just going to show you this–He held up a card on which were the figures–

"$141.00"

Later in his presentation, he asked, "How much will this save?"

Most of the listeners answered–

"$141.00"

I have seen this idea used with three ideas. The speaker had said, "This plan will save you–" Then he showed a visual–

1. Time
2. Labor, and
3. Money.

Later he asked the group, "What's your first saving?"

The listeners answered, "Time."

He asked them a similar question on, "What's the second?" Then, "What's the third?" Each time he got correct answers. The listeners had remembered three savings.

7. They Help You Clarify Your Points

The idea a picture shows can be grasped quickly. Words describing the same situation may require more concentration. You say your words and the listeners have an idea of what you mean. When you show your visual, they see what you mean. I heard a speaker say, "This photograph explains this idea clearly."

8. They Save Time

I saw a sales trainer ask the class, "How long do you think it would take you to describe these eight benefits of our product?" He got estimates of from eight minutes to fifteen minutes. Then he said, "I'll show you a TV commercial that covers those eight benefits. Note how much time it takes to cover them." He showed the commercial on the screen while one of the group timed the showing. The coverage took less than two minutes. "But the announcer used visuals," one man protested. "That's the point," the instructor said. "By using visuals you save time and it offers relief from your yak-yak." The visual allows the listener to grasp the idea faster and this allows the speaker to go on to his next point. Any few minutes you save in a talk is appreciated by the audience.

9. They Help You Stay on the Track

A talk illustrated with visuals guides you in covering your story. You have three benefits to cover. You show a chart that lists the three—

First, Time Saving
Second, Labor Saving
Third, Money Saving

Now everybody knows that you plan to cover three points.

Follow that chart with one that says—

First, how you save time

Now listeners know that you are talking about saving time. When you have finished your time story, you show a chart that reads—

Second, how you save labor

Listeners now know that you plan to take up your second point and talk about saving labor. When you have finished with that subject you show your third chart.

Third, how you save money

Listeners don't guess what you plan to talk about. The chart reminds them. And the chart reminds you so well that you are not likely to go off on a tangent about the ills of the world when a chart is reminding you of what you should be talking about.

10. They Make You Look Better

Listeners are inclined to think that the speaker who is well organized is competent. Your visual tells them that you are trying to help them see what you are talking about. It shows you are interested enough in them to want them to understand. Selection of a visual or its production calls for some homework. It tells the listener that you did some preparation. By showing two or three visuals in a row, you demonstrate that there is order in your presentation. We take advice from one we think has an orderly mind. We admire the competent and are willing to listen to them.

TEN TIPS ON USING VISUALS

You use a visual to help the listeners—
see what you are talking about, and
understand what you mean.

If your visuals don't help them see and understand, they are not doing their job for them or you. Here are some thoughts that will help you avoid common mistakes in the use of visuals.

1. *Keep Them Simple:* Make them easy to understand, easy to handle.
2. *Know What You Plan to Do and Say:* Showing a visual takes some doing and saying. Know what you are going to do and say as you show each visual.

3. *Apologies Won't Help:* Forget apologies and don't depreciate by stating, "This visual doesn't show exactly what I want you to see." If you admit the visual is not too good, how can you expect listeners to be interested in it?
4. *Make Large Enough to Be Seen:* If you want the listener to read what you show, use large enough type. Get enough light on the figures.
5. *Watch Crowded Charts:* Put too much on one visual and listeners will have difficulty following its message. If you think the chart is too crowded, put some of the data on a second chart. You may save listeners time by putting the message on three or four charts.
6. *Set Up Beforehand:* Think of the times you have seen meetings thrown into confusion when a speaker is introduced and starts to move chairs, tables and even people to set up his visuals. Avoid this disorder by setting up before the meeting starts.
7. *Slow Up:* A listener listens at one rate, sees at another. One value of a visual is that it helps take up the slack between listening and speaking speed. Don't rush your story. Leave your visual in sight until the listener sees what you are trying to tell him. Pause, be silent for a minute or so while he looks at what you show.
8. *Look at the Listeners, Not the Visual:* You have seen speakers show a visual, then stand talking to it. Your visual can't do anything about your plea. Talk to the people who can.
9. *Let Them Read in Silence:* You can do this with some visuals. If the visual is one that they can read, let them read without talk from you. A visual is supposed to cut the need for talk.
10. *Practice Using the Visual:* If it is a chart, practice bringing it into view. If it is a product or similar object, practice handling it. Fumbling with your visuals can get you rated as a fumbler.

TWO SENSES HELP MORE THAN ONE

Trainers know that a learner can absorb more if you tell him about a new building your company is building and then show him a picture of it. Describe the building in words and he may see little more than a lean-to. Show him the architect's drawing and he says, "Boy, that is something!" Trainers' tests show that we retain 20% of what we hear, 30% of what we see, but 50% of what we see and hear. You can use that second sense in about any talk. Show the cartoon and get your smile or laugh, uncover the photograph of the starving children to arouse emotion. Your visual will be remembered long after what you said is forgotten.

22

DRAMATICS CAN ASSIST YOUR OBJECTIVE

Feel it—show you feel it:
When you start to talk to a group you are

not a tape
not a recording

You are a living, breathing human being.
Show it.

When you try for humor show you enjoyed the incident you describe. Indicate you feel the listeners will enjoy it too. An old saying puts it, "Most smiles are started by another smile."

When you try to arouse feeling, show that you are enthusiastic angry, disturbed, sympathetic or whatever. You're wrought up and you feel the listeners should share your feelings about this right or this wrong.

A bit of histrionics can emphasize how you feel. You may say, "I'm not putting it on, I feel it." Ok, fine. But it helps to let yourself go. Let your feelings show and some of your emotion will transfer to your listeners. You help your humor or eloquence with your demonstrations of how you feel.

WHY YOU DON'T LIKE SPEECH READERS

Anybody can read the words from a manuscript, but how can you read words and show the emotion they stir in you? Think how the speech reader limits himself. The joke he reads won't generate as big a laugh as the one he speaks. By reading he may say exactly what he wants to say but he handicaps himself in using either eloquence or humor. He seems afraid to look up at you for fear he will lose his place. He increases the speed of his reading as he goes on. His effort seems to be more a job of finishing his script than reading it to you. The result–no cheers when he finishes. I saw a speaker use this device to get a bit of life into a speech reading job. He had inserted a number of gag stories in the manuscript. When he finished the first joke, he looked up, paused, and said, "That's supposed to be a joke, get it?" After that whenever he finished one of the jokes, he paused, looked up and asked, "Get it?" As he progressed his, "Get its?" got more response and gave him shots of humor that the read jokes didn't deserve. His "Get it?" shows how difficult it is to get a laugh with a joke you read.

YOUR ACTING EMPHASIZES YOUR FEELING

In training speakers I have found that the easiest actions for them to work with are–

Facial expressions

Gestures with arms, hands, fingers

Head motions

Voice manipulation

Of course, the four are combined in most emotions a speaker shows. When your face shows emotion, your hands help out, and your head and voice add their effects. To clarify how easy such motions are to develop, I'll deal with each separately.

FACIAL EXPRESSIONS ADD TO THE POWER OF YOUR WORDS

Some comedians show no expression as they rattle off jokes. That dead pan is a part of their humor. They have worked to perfect it. But if you want your gag or funny story to get a laugh, your best bet is to act as if the account is funny to you. You thought the gag was funny and your expression shows it. If you are enthusiastic about an idea, you get as much or more persuasion out of the emotion you show as you do from the words you speak. A speaker does not indicate we have to do some heavy thinking before we act when he says, "We must do this NOW."

WATCH THE SINGERS

In Chapter 4, I mentioned how the facial expressions of modern singers help communicate. As the singers sing about their lover disappearing with the no-good so-and-so, they don't seem to worry about melody. They concentrate on facial contortions and body gyrations to indicate the intensity of the hurt they are suffering. You know they are alive, but you wouldn't bet on how long they will live. Those singers, male and female, demonstrate the power of those facial expressions. The applause when the singer finishes shows how the listeners appreciate such histrionics.

Some of this same can help you get laughs, or sympathy for your cause. Expressions can show pain, amusement, surprise, disgust, horror, joy, disbelief, concern, interest, fatigue. These are moods you show every day. If your feelings are stirred to any emotion, why can't you show it as you speak about the incident that brought on the emotion.

THE SMILE IS THE EASIEST

I advise speakers to smile at the listeners before they say one word. One student asked, "With my knees knocking?" With those knees knocking, smile because listeners can't hear the knees and in a minute or so the knees will behave. Make that smile the first bit of dramatics in your speech. You'll be encouraged immediately because many of your audience will smile back. Many times that smile is a performance. You might perhaps rather be anywhere than speaking to this group on this subject at this time. But no matter how you feel about speaking, the smile helps make friends for you as you start. Most speakers say, "I am glad to be here." Ok, show it. What easier way than a smile?

THE SMILE AT MISFORTUNE WINS FRIENDS

You report that when you asked your secretary to go down to the machine and get you a pack of cigarettes she said, "I won't do it. The Surgeon General says cigarettes are injurious to your health." Secretaries aren't supposed to sound off like that. You'd like to tell her off. But don't report any telling off in a speech. Laugh at yourself and tell what happened when you went and got the cigarettes yourself. That's acting, isn't it? Let your face show how you felt. Shake your head a bit to indicate you are asking, "What's the world coming to?" In using humor the successful speaker does much of this type of laughing at himself.

BUILD UP YOUR DISCOMFITURE AND THE LISTENERS LAUGH

Let's say you ask the cop who stopped you because you ran through a stop sign that was almost invisible, "Don't a lot of drivers fail to see that sign?" He retorts, "No, not many morons drive this street." A bit of histrionics here will indicate that you wonder which school of law enforcement teaches comments like this. But you shrug off the insult. Let's say that when your secretary refused to go get the cigarettes you started after them yourself. On the way you ran into your boss, who asked you to step into a vacant office. After he closed the door he asked, "How would you feel if I stole your secretary?" You asked, "For a day or two?" He says, "No, for keeps." You're in trouble now. It is a promotion for the secretary, but she'll think you got rid of her because she wouldn't go for your cigarettes." A bit of histrionics will make that story more humorous. Watch the next speaker you hear telling of something embarrassing that happened to him. What acting helps the story to seem more humorous? Set backs batter your ego, Ok, let your face show it. Tell it like it happened, how you felt about it, and let your embarrassment, frustration, or whatever will, show on your face.

GESTURES SHOW YOU ARE ALIVE

In the early days of instruction in public speaking, gestures were taught. Standard gestures showed certain emotions.

Today's instructors say that the gestures come naturally. I once saw Phil Douglas, a National League pitcher of John McGraw's New York Giants, wave his gloved hand towards the plate umpire. That gesture with a negative shake of Phil's head said more about the pitcher's opinion of the umpire's judgment on balls and strikes than thousands of words. That action came naturally. It called for no rehearsal.

YOU'LL LEARN BY WATCHING GREAT SPEAKERS

Last week on TV I watched Rev. Billy Graham preach one of his sermons to thousands in an outdoor stadium. If I hadn't heard one word, I would have known it was a strong speech. His face, his hands, his arms told me he was aroused.

Here are some of his motions–

he held up one hand
pointed with one finger
moved his hands continuously
held his arms out, up, down
he made a circle with one hand to illustrate a great area
clasped his hands
held hands out with palms down
held his hands above his head, fingers open
closed the open fingers into a fist

I say that these are some of his gestures, there were more, and I imagine that if I showed that list to Mr. Graham, he would ask, "Did I do all of those things?" He did, and I made notes as he did them. Another speaker might have leaned on the lectern and mouthed the same words, but he wouldn't have moved the listeners to get on their feet, march down front of the speaker and declare themselves.

MOVEMENT TELEGRAPHS YOUR INTEREST

The movements indicated that Mr. Graham was trying to share his great message with his listeners. The gestures emphasized the depth of his commitment. He demonstrated that when you feel about a subject you can't stand still like a clothing store dummy and talk about it. Your feelings bring on action–your arms, your hands, your whole being spring to life. Do you think Patrick Henry's hands were in his pockets when he shouted, "Give me liberty or give me death?"

GESTURES COME NATURALLY TO YOU

You've heard the expression, "Tie that guy's hands behind him and he wouldn't be able to talk." Students in my speaking groups have told me, "I don't go in for gestures." I ask, "Why not?" They say, "I'd feel conscious making them." I have asked students who said they couldn't use gestures to take a subject in which they had strong feelings and make a two-minute speech on it. I ask the class to make count the times the speaker has used hands or arms during the two minutes. All of the speakers use gestures, just as the rest of us do when our feelings take over. Photographers have snapped me while speaking to audiences and have caught me with my hands above my head. I wouldn't believe I had reached to high heaven at any point in the speech, but the photograph was proof. Next time you explain something to a child, watch your hands. This noon at lunch, check how you emphasize what you say with hand motions. You'll find that you use a lot of motion every day.

SIGN LANGUAGE HELPS EXPLAIN

You wave to greet another, you clap your hands to indicate approval, you make a "V" with two fingers to indicate hooray for our side. The ok sign with the circle and three fingers shows agreement. Then think of these gestures–

Your index finger over your lips to ask for quiet

Your hand cupped behind your ear saying you don't hear

Your index finger beckons another

The same finger pointed at a door indicates the other is to exit.

Ask a child, "How many years are you?" The youngster holds up two, three or four fingers. The tot may not know how to say the numbers, but he has learned how to communicate. Develop this tendency to use your hands when you speak. With most of us it comes naturally. I heard a speaker say, "One day we had a prosperous business, that night, fire. Everything went up–POUF." As he said that last word his hands went up to indicate an explosion. Then he repeated, "Business, profits, hopes, dreams, all—Pouf." Again the hands went high.

YOUR HANDS HELP COMMUNICATE YOUR FEELINGS

Our hands have developed certain motions to show our feelings. We may not be conscious of these motions that come naturally. Try this experiment—

1. Say, "We Can Do Nothing." What do your hands do? Mine seem to fall palms up in front of me, an indication of helplessness.

2. Say, "They Can't Do That to Us." Do your hands indicate you are ready to fight? Do they help show you are ready to lower the boom, to pick up a banner and join the march? How do they help show how you feel?

3. Say, "May the Lord Strike Me Dead if This Isn't True." Do your hands indicate that you are trying to ward off a blow? Or do they show you are confident that no bolt of lightning is on its way. I saw one speaker raise his hands, fingers outstretched as if he were welcoming such a blow. A more dramatic speaker might tear open his collar and pull his shirt aside to bare his chest for the bolt. That would be effective, but do you need all of that?

YOUR HEAD ADDS TO YOUR MESSAGE

Use your head. You hear that advice again and again. Speaking instructors tell you, "Move your head, look at the people in front of you, at the right and at the left." Too many speakers look straight ahead as they talk on. The movements of the head to right and left help those you look at feel that you are also talking to them.

You nod your head to say, "Yes."
You shake it to say, "No."

You go through these motions many times in a day. Both are useful in your speaking. Say, "We want this, don't we?" Nod your head as you say the words and many of the listeners will nod in agreement. Say, "We will never accept this deal." Shake your head to say "No" as you say it and some listeners will shake their heads to indicate that they are with you.

YOUR HEAD MOVES NATURALLY

I saw a speaker throw his hands above his head as he appealed to the God above and what did his head do? It turned up as he looked towards the ceiling as if he expected immediate arrival of the help that he solicited from on high. If that same speaker had consigned an idea to the nether regions, I as sure that he would have looked down to follow the progress of the idea to perdition. These movements come naturally and they add to the message of the words used with them.

YOUR VOICE GIVES ITS LIFT

The three requirements of voice use are–

1. Loud enough for the listeners to hear
2. Slow enough for them to understand, and
3. Enunciation that helps clarify every word and sentence.

You can see the sense in these requirements. But there are other aids your voice can give you. It can indicate your excitement. It can show your frustration, enthusiasm. You can speak louder, softer, shout, whisper. You have seen the performer move closer to the footlights, cup his hand beside his mouth to indicate he didn't want the people backstage to hear what he said. He probably didn't lower his voice much, but his preparation made you feel that he did. This bit of acting can be used in both comedy and eloquence.

LET THE PAUSE WORK FOR YOU

The pause has been mentioned before. You ask a question and pause as if you expected an answer. That's acting, isn't it? Your urge is to talk on and show you know the answer. But the pause gives listeners a moment to think about the answer. Praise an activity and it is difficult to keep your approval out of your voice. Sit on a thumbtack and your howl indicates the hurt. Maybe your words help, but the emotion put into how you say those words comes more from the hurt. Give your voice an opportunity. Let it show your feelings. Hit hard on the words that emphasize how you feel. Forget the deadly monotone. When you try to persuade, raise your voice, lower it, shout, whisper. The tone of your voice can help more than you imagine.

YOUR MIRROR CAN HELP IMPROVE YOUR HISTRIONICS

Make the request, "Mirror, mirror on the wall, how do I look doing it all?" Shake your head as you might when you wanted a "No" agreement. Do you think your head shaking from side to side would indicate you were against the plan? If not, change your way of shaking your head until you feel it is indicating what you want. Check the other motions you use naturally—hands, arms, body. Do they help your message? You'll find that some of your facial expressions do not indicate the emotion you thought they did. One speaker told me, "I smiled at myself in a mirror and I looked like a sick calf." "What did you do?" I asked. "I rubbed my hands on my cheeks, loosened my facial muscles, and tried again. This time I smiled. "To check hands and arms, talk a part of your speech to the person in the mirror and let your hands and arms do what they would do naturally. Are the motions what you thought, or do some of them look awkward? Try again and again until you feel the gestures are graceful. If your hands seem too active, cut some of the movement. The listener may become more interested in watching those hands than in understanding what you say. Then, too, there is no need to go overboard; you are not trying for an Academy Award.

"WHAT COMES NATURALLY" IS BEST

In suggesting you do a bit of histrionics, I'm asking you to do what you do every day. When you get angry, you show it, when you enjoy a joke you laugh. When you are fatigued or worried a friend may ask, "You feeling ok?" Most of us react this way. It's normal to show our feelings and we like to listen to, do business with, and follow the lead of normal people. Let your emotions show in your face and your voice, emphasize how you feel with your hands, arms and head, and you'll give your humor and eloquence more believability.

23

AUDIENCE PARTICIPATION GETS LAUGHS OR AROUSES EMOTION

The M.C. says, "Give the little girl a hand."

And the audience applauds with gusto.

Why, because we all like to get into the act.

You've seen this desire used to get laughs.

Even the simple request that each member of the audience shake hands with the persons in the next chairs gets a smile and a laugh.

You've seen it used to arouse emotion. One of the audience gives a sample solicitation and testifies to the success in using it for the fund drive. The listener hears and says, "If that girl can do it, I can too." The demonstration gave the listener the assurance that the solicitation was easier to do than it seemed.

In the chapters ahead I have listed the types of material that listeners like to hear. Here are suggestions as to how to use audience participation with each type.

WITH THE STORY

Give the audience a part in telling the story and it will be more enjoyable to them. Here is a demonstration with this one liner–

"The argument you won from your wife isn't over yet."

You like this line, you think it will be funny to this group and so you plan to use it. But it is just ten words. It will take about six seconds to say it. You'd like to give it a bit more time to sink in. OK, how about this procedure:

You ask the question,

"How many of you gentlemen ever won an argument from your wife?"

You pause, then ask, "Hold up your hand if you have."

You get a show of hands. Just a few and some of these are bragging. Then you say, "Let me tell you something, gentlemen,–" *Pause*–"That argument isn't over yet."

Listeners' enjoyment of the gag is increased because you let them help you make the point. To emphasize the laugh line in telling a funny story, I ask, "What do you think the character said?"

I pause while the listeners try to think what the character said. If one blurts out what he said, you perhaps may have a bigger laugh than you would get with your original line. In such a case, let them laugh and then use your line. This gives you two laughs and allows the listeners to compare the two lines.

To Arouse Emotion

The speaker who talks for the boys club brings a member of the club along with him. At the proper time the boy is introduced and asked to tell what the club means to him. After hearing the youngster tell his story the listeners are more inclined to give to the cause.

In one such presentation a listener asked, "What do you boys need most at your camp?"

Without hesitation the boy replied, "Room for more kids." That "room for more kids" was the most powerful argument for the cause.

Any Testimony Helps: A similar effect can be produced by having one of your club members testify to what he saw and heard when he spent one day and a night at the boys camp. You can tell the story, but you are prepared. The one you bring on to help is not as well prepared, he wants to help though, and his words may carry more conviction than yours. His willingness to help shows in his talk and makes the non-helpers ask, "What can I do?"

WITH CONVERSATION

When the speaker opens the meeting for questions you get conversation. A listener asks a question. The speaker answers it. Since so many of the audience try for laughs, many questions bring smiles. The same is true when the club member questions a policy that the club governors have set up. He may use strong language in expressing his opposition. A member of the audience shouts, "Yea, Yea." This can be the start of a rhubarb and such disturbances are enjoyed by both participants and listeners.

Making Conversation with No Words

I do one audience participation bit to help prove that a man can say a lot with no words at all. I ask four men to stand beside me. Then I ask the first to hold his index finger vertically in front of his lips. I ask the listeners, "What is he saying?" A number shout, "Silence." I then say, "And he hasn't said a word, has he?" The next fellow I have cup his hand behind his ear. I then ask, "What's he saying?" More listeners answer, "Louder." Again I ask, "He hasn't said a word, has he?" I then ask the third man to beckon with his index finger. Again I ask, "What is he saying?" The group answers, "Come here." I repeat, "He hasn't said a word, has he?" I have the last man point at the door. I ask, "What's he saying." The group calls, "Get out." Again I ask, "He hasn't said a word, has he?" This stunt illustrates the point that most of us talk too much. These actions were mentioned in Chapter 22, as a bit of histrionics, but by demonstrating with the four men, the group has a better chance of remembering the point. The conversation back and forth gives the stunt life. Any bit of conversation can be used to arouse emotion. It is the type of participation you need when you shout, "Let's go burn down the Bastile!"

USE WITH NEWS

Used with news, audience participation comes naturally. Let's say you read an item from your newspaper. You ask, "How many read that item?" A number of the listeners will indicate they read the bit, and you are on common ground with them. Others will think, "I missed it." They will be interested in hearing more about this piece they missed. Mention of a bit of news has drawn the listeners closer to you.

For Humor: You read in the paper that a Judge told a wife she couldn't force her husband to live in a tree." The item sounds far out, but there are many such. You tell about the husband hauled into court for hitting his wife. The judge asked how it happened, the man said, "She was yapping at me, and I just hauled off and socked her in the puss."

"That's all?" the judge asked.

"That's all," the husband agreed.

"What happened then?" the judge went on.

"Well, judge, I socked her, and you may not believe this, but that's the last thing I remember."

Now you ask the question, "How many of you fellows have lived through emergencies when you would have liked to sock your wife?" Maybe you won't get a single affirmative but you'll get a lot of smiles. After a pause, while you wait for a confession you say, "This item explains why it is a good idea to use discretion."

Participation Aids Eloquence: I saw a speaker use this idea. He was talking to a luncheon club about contributing to relief of an area that had been hit by a tornado. The news report said that 70% of the people had been killed or disabled. The room was set up ten people at each round table. He asked three persons at each table to stand. He said, "I tell you 70% and you can't picture it. But here you can see it. You people sitting are dead or disabled. You three standing have to take care of the mess. You'd need help, wouldn't you?"

The seven sitting would get the idea, "This could have happened to me." The three standing would ask, "How can we handle the job?" All feel the crisis is real. It's no longer a newspaper or TV story. All agree each should do something about it. Now the speaker tells them what to do. This speaker had learned that by putting his listeners in the picture, he could get greater response.

POSSESSIONS MAKE GOOD PARTICIPATION TOOLS

The speaker asks how many have watches. Then he asks each to look at his watch for thirty seconds. In ten seconds he asks, "What are we doing?" Someone responds, "We're looking at our watches." He says, "And we're wasting time." Then he brings up his theme: "Time is the most valuable possession we have and here we are frittering it away, watching a second hand ticking off seconds we will never get back." The subject of this talk was, "Your income depends on how well you manage your time."

In my talks I use a pencil to help in a number of ways. One idea it helps demonstrate is that it is difficult to teach a man anything, even highly intelligent people such as the listeners. I demonstrate a four-count exercise with my pencil. I say, "That is an easy exercise to do, isn't it?" When I get agreement, I say, "Now I'm going to show how difficult it is to teach that exercise to you, a highly intelligent group." The highly intelligent gets a smile, of course. I then ask each of them to get out a pencil or pen and try to follow what I do. At the count of one, I hold the pencil horizontally in front of my face, right hand at right. At the count of two, I move the hands to a vertical position, right hand on bottom, at three I move the pencil to a horizontal position again, with the right hand at right, at four I move it back to vertical with the right hand on top. I have them follow me in the exercise twice. Then I ask them to do it as I count. A goodly number of the listeners can't follow this routine. I express disgust at their failure. I go on, "If I drill you ten times on this routine, about 80% of you will get it right, but a certain percentage of you are morons and will never get it right." Insult humor, yes, but no one takes offense because all of them feel the slur applies to a listener nearby who they saw get the exercise balled up.

Humor and Eloquence in One Bit: A speaker said, "Today at lunch everybody spilled a bit of gravy on his tie. Look at your tie and find yours." When each has looked, he asks, "You didn't notice that spot until now, did you? And it happened right under your nose." Now he ties the "didn't know it" idea into his premise that we go along unaware of what the enemy is doing to us. The necktie bit has its humor, some are looking for something that isn't there, others find the damage. But all are set up for the story that proves his premise about the enemy.

FIGURES MAKE GOOD AUDIENCE BAIT

For Humor: The humor in figures comes mainly from the use of the ridiculous or exaggeration. I heard a home economist explaining the ingredients in her fancy dessert as she added and mixed them ask, "What do you think we add now?" Her male shill in the audience called, "One fourteen ounce bottle of catsup." "Why catsup, and why so much," she asked. "I like catsup," the man replied. The exchange brought a laugh. In Chapter 20 I used, "The fried chicken's good, but they give you thirteen pieces." Getting the listeners in may take some arranging, but it helps.

For Eloquence: When talking against a new tax, you might estimate what the new tax is going to cost each of your listeners. You arouse more interest by proposing, "Take a pencil now and write down what this is going to cost you." You may tell them, "It is going to cost you at least 33 dollars," and the amount may register. But when they write $33 and study the figure, they become convinced that it is too much. And they are more willing to do what you suggest to protest the tax. Any request to write something or figure a problem is a challenge that an audience will accept. I am surprised at how many of an audience will reach for pen and paper when I ask, "Write this down, please." It helps the bit if I get after the ones who didn't respond and ask them to write. This willingness can be expanded, have them write two or three numbers and add them. Then ask one, "What answer did you get?" When you get an answer, ask, "Anybody get a different answer?" Listeners like this kind of a drill and they are happy that you asked them to take part.

THERE IS BOTH HUMOR AND ELOQUENCE IN VISUALS

Show a cartoon and you inject some humor. Show a sad picture and you arouse an emotion. On the front page of my newspaper, I found a photo of a small girl. The headline of the caption was "Hungry Eyes." The type went on, "This young girl is watching people starving all around her." The picture was well chosen, the girl looked at you with listless eyes. She seemed to have lost all hope. But her eyes were open, they stared at you. If you had any heart you would want to help this child. A speaker could bring the listeners into this by holding up the visual and asking the listeners to write a caption. If the photo is too small to show, have it passed around and ask each listener to write a caption for it. If possible have a copy of the visual for each. When you get the captions back, read them or have listeners read their answers. This procedure could be worked with a cartoon or with the photo "Hungry Eyes." You might offer a prize for the caption or title the group votes best. As you read this outline think of such stunts. Try any of them. Many audience participation efforts don't work the first time speakers try them. But if they keep asking, the group sees they mean to get help and it eventually comes through. Let's say you used the photo "Hungry Eyes" to help get contributions for the Red Cross or the Missionary Relief Fund of your church. You show the photograph and ask one, "What do you think we should do to help?" When one is finished, ask another. Listeners want to help, let them add punch to your appeal.

THERE IS COMEDY OR TRAGEDY IN DRAMATICS

At any fund-raising session it is possible to bring up two members of the audience and have one act as the solicitor, the other as the prospective giver. The solicitor uses the prepared materials to make the solicitation. The prospect gives the objections for which answers have been provided, the solicitor answers each with the standard answers. Of course, such a demonstration goes over better if the two shills have rehearsed.

In a talk on common courtesy I heard a speaker stage a drill on having the listeners say, "Please," and "Thank you." He managed the drill by saying, "I'm going to count three and when I finish, I want you to say *'Please.'* " He counted one, two, three, and his group said *"Please."* He got almost 100% cooperation. He asked, "Does that sound strange coming from you?" That line brought a laugh. Next he handled *"Thank you"* in the same way. In asking an audience to say anything it is well to have them say it a number of times. After the first try say, "We can do better than that." Now try it again. A second try will get more participation, a third will get even more.

A speaker on better English handled the words
"Yes,"
"No,"
"You" and the ending,
"ing"
in a similar fashion. The premise was that if the listeners handled these words and the ending properly, they could improve their language. All of these stunt type demonstrations strengthened the speaker's story. Most of the ones you hear are originals developed by the speaker. If you want to emphasize a point, work out a plan to have the listeners help you emphasize it.

How to Make Your Participation Stunt Produce Humor or Emotion

Think of these angles.

1. Have an objective. If you want a laugh, concentrate on the laugh. If you want to arouse an emotion, stick to that objective.
2. Plan what you want the listeners to do. If it is a show of hands, figure how high you want those hands raised.
3. Know what you will say, what you will do. Rehearse.
4. When you have the listeners do the task, explain what you have proven by it.
5. Compliment the group on how well they have performed. This is more important with the single individual.

6. If the participant doesn't do well in a task, cover foı him, explain you put him on the spot.
7. Treat all helpers with respect, ask for applause at the finish. Never crack jokes at a participant.
8. In group demonstrations insist that all take part. Get after the ones who aren't cooperating. Audiences love your chiding of the ones who feel too important to take part.

Cater to the Listener

Listeners want to take part. They enjoy helping. And in so many cases you can get your laugh or arouse emotion by giving them a job to do. Have no fear of failure, ask for help and you'll be surprised at how much you can get. Listeners like to be made a part of your story. They like it because it is different from the usual speaker. One successful speaker advised, "If you want a standing ovation at the end of your speech, work up a stunt that has the listeners on their feet at the end. Here is an example. The speaker says, "Look around at the people in the room, will you please. There is fatigue on every face, everybody seems to have had it, you oldsters look every year your age, you young people don't look so hot either. Now will you all stand up. Raise your hands above your head. After I count three, start wiggling your fingers like this–One, two, three–wiggle." The fingers wiggle, a smile lights every face. After about thirty seconds the speaker says, "Now, sit down, please, look around you, everybody's alert, and Mr. Chairman, while they are in that condition, I give them back to you." The speaker sits down, but the listeners are back on their feet, applauding.

He built his standing ovation, didn't he? The group loves such a stunt, he is talking about them, he brings them into his talk, he demonstrates a remedy that banishes their fatigue, and best of all, from their standpoint, he ends his speech.

Part Four

HOW TO USE HUMOR AND ELOQUENCE TO ASSURE A GOOD IMPRESSION

All through the book the value of impression has been stressed. Your objective is to make as good an impression as possible. Make a good talk and listeners get the impression you desire them to join up, to work, to donate, to pick up a banner and follow you in the parade.

The chapters in this part of the book cover techniques that are important in broadcasting that good impression—

First, the start of your speech—a good start builds rapport and anticipation.

Second, the end of your speech, a good ending gives the listeners the impression they take home.

Third, how your handling of material gives listeners a picture that inspires confidence in you.

Speakers who have developed skill in these three areas advance to better jobs in business or the professions. They are able to give more help in religious, civic, or fraternal work. They become better citizens, and in most cases, ability to use humor and eloquence adds the polish that gives them this high rating.

24

HOW TO START WITH HUMOR OR ELOQUENCE

There are a number of ways to start a speech that will–

- Get attention
- Arouse interest,
- Picture you as one of the group, and,
- Indicate that you offer something they want.

The previous chapters have mentioned many of these starts. Think of–

1. The "On my way here" start
2. A story about the chairman's conversation with you.
3. A story about you and the family–the spouse and kids.

4. Accounts of contacts with your boss or your secretary
5. Your illogical frustrations as you made logical moves

Then there are reports on standard starts–

6. The question
7. Quotations
8. A bit of poetry
9. The explanation of what you are to talk about, and not cover
10. The use of the meeting theme
11. The showing of a visual
12. The stunt.

Every one of these starts can be used to produce humor or eloquence.

Let's examine how these different starts are used:

1. *Tell What Happened "On My Way Here" Start:* This is the standard vaudeville comedian's start. Something happened to the speaker on the way to the hall. The happening does not have to be important. Let's say the man at the door taking tickets wouldn't let you into the hall without an admission ticket. He kept you waiting until the chairman came to recognize you. When you argued, the worthy said, "You'd be surprised, Mister, at the number of creeps that try to talk their way past me." This O.M.W.H. start is usually a bit of comedy, but it can be used to arouse emotion. The speaker walked through a part of the ghetto on the way to the hall. What he saw, and how he described his feelings arouse emotion. The audience in the hall in evening clothes, just one block away a world in rags and filth and hunger. "You cringe from contact with such people," he states. "Yet these too are our brothers." Those who agree with the statement have one feeling, those who disagree have another. But the story arouses an emotion in all.

2. *Talk about the Chairman, the Committee, a Friend in the Group:* In this type you say, "I asked the Chairman what was

the intelligence quotient of this group. I'm not going to tell you how he rated you for if I told you true, I'm sure that he would be chairman no longer." Such starts have been mentioned all through the book, and mostly for humor, but supposing the speaker said, "Your chairman said I had a busy schedule, and I have. It is difficult to fit in another talk. But I'll tell you this: any time I get a chance to assist in a tribute to Chuck Whosis, I'll travel the three hundred miles to help. And you know why, you are Chuck's friends. You have seen what Chuck has done for his fellow men." Follow this with a list of the jobs Chuck has handled and you are certain to stir emotion.

3. *Borrow from Your Family:* Your spouse, the kids, the uncles and aunts, the in-laws. All can help you get that start. Your high school son says, "Mom, why would anyone ask you to lecture to them?" Your spouse asks, "What do you know about that subject?" Listeners relate to such conversations, it is what they hear at home. As they laugh at your accounts maybe they will learn a bit about laughing at their own similar setbacks. A mother told of coming home from a meeting and finding her two teenagers lying on the floor playing peggity. "The game board is on the floor in the middle of the two, one boy is spread out six feet to the north, the other six feet to the south. You can imagine how much room that left me to go through that room. I started to scream at them and then held up. Those boys lived here, this was their home as much as mine. This is a fact we are inclined to forget. Maybe they could find a place to play their game, that wouldn't require a whole room. But they are within their rights doing what they were doing. 'Who's winning?' I asked and stepped over them and I like to think I earned some pearls in my crown." You've had similar situations in your home with your kids, and you can make points with how you handled it. Her premise was that kids have rights, and she clearly introduced it and gave us a lecture on it without mentioning our faults.

4. *Tell About Your Boss:* At times mentioning the boss might come under the head of living dangerously. If the boss doesn't laugh at his own foibles when he speaks, he may not see

anything funny in your discussion of them. I heard a speaker start, "When my boss gets back from a meeting he tells me the stories the speaker used. As a good secretary I listen. Most of his stories are blah, but just yesterday he came back with one that made me laugh." Built up by that introduction she has listeners asking, "What was the story?" The story was humorous, but it could have been one to arouse the emotions. Another similar introduction I heard was, "My boss is a genius, but sometimes he slips up." I heard a speaker say, "Let's imagine that as your chairman finished my introduction and I stood to speak, six masked men armed with automatic rifles rushed into this room. The rifles covered every one as the leader said, "Stand–all of you. Put all your valuables on the table in front of you, money, wallets, watches, rings, then reach your hands above your heads. A diner shouts, 'The hell with you.' One of the gang hits the offender over the head with a rifle, the protester falls to the floor. The rest of you rush to follow orders." The speaker paused, then said, "That's what this world is coming to today–we are a peace-loving people–but violence is breaking out among us. Today violence has become a way of life." Some listeners may think this opening is a gag, but all would feel some emotion at the part that violence plays in our current lives–muggings, hold ups, murders, kidnapping, sky jacking.

5. *Bring on Your Secretary:* The gag says that an executive needs a wife to tell him what to do, and a secretary to do it for him. I used the example of the secretary who refused to get a pack of cigarettes for her boss because they were dangerous to his health. I heard an executive say, "My secretary is on vacation, and they gave me a girl from Central Steno to fill in." You know when you hear this that the poor speaker is in trouble. A secretary can do anything, say anything, to break up the peaceful routine. Then she can so run your office that you are free of all problems. I heard one speaker tell how after his secretary had typed his speech, he asked, "What did you think of it." "I wish you wouldn't use that word 'lousy' " she said. "Why?" he asked. "Ever had lice?" she asked. "No," he answered. "Well, some listener may have had and the reference would bring back painful memories." The executive's secretary

is so much a part of an executive's life that talk about her puts listeners in the area where they live. One executive told about his secretary having asked him not to wear a bow tie to the office. He asked why and she said, "I think it makes you look like a sissy." "You don't want to work for a sissy?" he asked. "No, it's not that," she said. He related how he quit wearing bow ties, and then one day his wife examining his assortment of ties, asked, "Why don't you wear one of these nice bow ties, Frank?" Speech material, isn't it?

6. *Offer a Bit of Poetry:* We are all fond of poetry, particularly the poem that rhymes. I use one that goes,

> I have come to the conclusion,
> After giving it a test,
> That of all my wife's relations,
> I like myself the best.

This bit is used in a unit that tells listeners to shape their speeches to tell audiences what they gain. The poetry can be slanted at either humor or eloquence. Without too much research you can find bits of poetry that will help you introduce any subject. I offer these suggestions:

a. *Use Short Pieces:* You may lose the listener with a longer bit. The one quoted is about the right length.

b. *Use the Rhyming:* Listeners like rhymes. At the start of your speech they think you might give with a ponderous thought. Perhaps you cross them with the rhyme, but they will like it.

c. *Use the Old Friends:* Don't confuse. In a unit on the value of a smile I use–

> The one worth while
> Is the one who can smile

The verse is so familiar that the audience automatically fills in the next line and agrees with the thought.

d. *Use the Easy-to-Understand:* Ones that everybody knows are best. Throughout the book I have used many quotes that I feel are old friends of mine. Most of them are also friends of the listener.

7. *Bring in Your Frustrations:* Tell about them but be sure you laugh at them. The trouble getting to the scene is popular. You started to make this trip from Mansfield, Ohio, to London, Ontario. It was a simple trip, a flight to Cleveland, then across the lake to London. The plane took off, but halfway to Cleveland it was turned back, storms had closed the Cleveland airport. When the plane got back, Mansfield airport was closed in, and you were put off the plane at Columbus, Ohio. You are now sixty miles further away from your destination. You get on a plane for Detroit, the airport there is clear. You land and go to a hotel. The next morning you take a train to London. Add the telephoning you have to do to advise everybody where you are. Then don't forget the ride in a police car to the place of the dinner, through sleet and snow, on icy roads, that are closed to ordinary traffic. Mention the lieutenant of Canadian police that chauffered the car. This is frustration, but don't cry about it. Remember, "Laugh and the listener laughs at you." How about the young executive that had to make the important presentation to the budget committee of his company. He got dolled up for the occasion, and the luncheon waitress spilled a bowl of soup on his new coat. Or the father who wanted to wear a special blue shirt and found that his teenage son was already gone with it. Listeners laugh at your frustrations, so present them with a smile. The frustrations may hurt but smile through the tears. You don't want the audience to classify you as a crab, do you?

8. *Blast the Politicians:* These sturdy worthies are always worth a whack. The bureaucrats that built the three houses for one million dollars were mentioned. They laid themselves wide open to attack. The Congress raises its pay. You think it would be a good idea to start a campaign to vote against every elected official who took such a raise. Uncle Sugar gives money for arms to emerging nations. They argue that these nations should be helped. You agree we should help in disasters to relieve hunger and protect health. But why give them the arms to shoot at the neighboring nations as they emerge? The city income tax

you voted for because it was supposed to be used to keep the streets in repair, then after a short time is used for all manner of handouts. The actions are to some humorous, tragic to others.

9. *Appeal with an Arousing Question:* You start, "Let's assume you were on a committee that was given one million dollars to build houses for the poor. Got that? You have one million dollars to spend. How many houses could you build?" You have given the listeners the problem. Give them a few seconds to consider. Then tell the story of the bureaucrats who were given that million dollars and came up with three fourteen thousand dollar houses. Your six-year-old nephew could have done better. You can make this opening more personal by asking, "How many of you have high blood pressure?" or "How many of you are making enough money?" "How many of you are working too hard?" "How many like your boss?" Questions at the start get attention. And if they probe a subject that is of interest to all, you have either the laugh or the bit of emotion that you planned for.

10. *Brighten with a Quotation:* It can be good for either humor or eloquence. The line, "Do a little more each day than is expected of you," could be your theme for an inspirational talk. But if you added a few words, you have a humorous bit, "Do a little more than is expected of you each day and it won't be long until a little more will be expected of you." In using quotations of the great I suggest you use a well-known author or person. –Shakespeare, Lincoln, F.D.R., J.F.K. Use the ancients, but try to stick to the better known names among them–Socrates, Sophocles, Cato. The "Quotation" books offer hundreds of ideas that can be used. In the two books near my office desk there are close to two thousand quotations. My practice when I need a quotation on a certain subject is to look in the index of these books, make notes of the locations of the quotes on the subject, look up the page numbers, and write out the quote. Usually I find five to ten that have possibilities.

11. *Explain What You Will Talk About:* The speaker starts, "One of the members asked me what I was going to talk about. My answer was, 'About three minutes.' " You might start. "I

plan to talk about three things–first, how to save time, second, how to save labor, and third, how to save money." The other day I heard a lawyer say, "I'm not going to talk about the right of this law or how I feel about it. I'm going to cover the law as it is written and what the courts have decided it means." This explains why the speaker may not cover angles that listeners thought might be covered. The speaker who lost the button off his overcoat could use that incident to make a point on the indifference of sales people. That need of a button could lead to an explanation of why everyone of the listeners were hurt by such indifference. That indifference means lost sales at a time when only more sales will help the economy. There is always the chance of humor in such a situation, all he needs is to report that his ten-year-old son said, "Quit worrying about it, Dad, use a safety pin. That's what I do."

12. *Shock with a Startling Statement:* Start with, "One year from today three of you listeners will have been smashed up in automobile accidents." You have shocked listeners into attention for even though you explain that you are using averages, they want to hear how they can be counted out of that unlucky three. You are favoring fastening seat belts but start, "Fasten your seat belts," and they say, "Here we go again." The startling statement about the wise ones, who because they were sitting on their seat belts, are now statistics has a better chance of grabbing attention. You might start, "Just this morning after twenty-three years of marriage, my wife and I decided to get a divorce." There are two shocks here. One, "Why are you telling us about it?" and, two, "What happened this morning that hasn't happened hundreds of times before?" Such a statement lends itself to humor. Supposing you add, "Every Thursday morning we feel like getting a divorce.–*Pause*–That's the morning she burns the toast."

13. *Use a Visual:* Stick the message in their eyes. I mentioned the photograph, "Hungry Eyes." Mighty few of us have ever been hungry through a whole day in our lives. When a speaker shows a picture of men, women and children starving we all want to do what we can to help alleviate the situation. A visual

can get a laugh. Remember the picture of the sad sack in a box, with the headline, "People are no damn good." The speaker who started by saying that he was going to explain how the listeners could save time, labor and money, could have had those three words printed on a chart he showed. Such a chart would have increased the value of the words. A visual at the start of your talk tells the audience that you are not going to try to sway them with words alone. A visual tells listeners that you have done some homework, you have spent some time preparing. The same message in words gives them no assurance.

14. *Startle with a Stunt:* You have seen the speaker take his place behind the lectern. In his hands he holds a number of typed pages. He takes great care in arranging these on the lectern. He says, "Ladies and gentlemen—" Perhaps he reads a sentence. Then he takes the typed pages and starts tearing them in small pieces. He throws the pieces in the air, perhaps so that some of them fall on his head. He makes some derogatory remarks about the material. It may be, "This is the speech the boss told me to give but he won't be here to hear me and so you get a break." Such a stunt gets attention, listeners see promise in it. The speaker is not going to be dull and boring, a stunt start tells them this.

I use a stunt that asks the group to clap three times at the start. I explain, "This is to see how well you can applaud. A number of times during this speech you will want to applaud and I am testing to see that you are prepared." I mentioned having the group at the luncheon meeting inspecting their ties to see if they spilled gravy on them. Listeners go for these stunts, and with planning you can work the stunt to help you make any point, either humorous or emotional. The secret of success of any stunt is planning—what you say—what you want the participants to do—what you do to explain.

The stunt start may be valuable if you come on late in the meeting and the audience is tired. It awakens them and gives you a better chance to give thought to your message.

Use Your Standard Start: Most experienced speakers have a standard start. I heard one speaker say, "I have come from Boston, and I want to say at the start that some things you have heard about Boston are not true. For instance, people from Boston don't think that if anything is fun it is a sin." A standard start can help a speaker get going. It need be no more than one short paragraph. Memorize the words, rehearse the action, and you have a smooth start that can be either humorous or eloquent.

THESE TIPS HELP ANY START

Smile at the Listeners: Pause at the start before you say one word and smile at this group. In my book *How to Write a Speech* I suggest the first word you write be *Smile.* Pause and smile.

Don't Rush: Most speakers are so anxious to get started that they rush to take off and blurt out the opening sentences, even if the sentence has a similar meaning to "Rome wasn't built in one day." Act composed, even if you are jittery. Take your time and that fright will take care of itself.

Look over the Whole Audience: A leisurely start allows you to look over the group. Act as if you wondered who came. All listeners want to be included and you want to include them. Look at one group throughout your speech and others resent it.

YOU CAN START WITH HUMOR OR ELOQUENCE

The examples given show how easy it is to use either a humorous or eloquent start. And each example should spark ideas for similar starts that you can develop. Try the ideas I mentioned or ones you develop. You'll soon get so good at it, that listeners will rate you as a better speaker.

25

SIXTEEN WAYS TO END YOUR SPEECH WITH HUMOR OR ELOQUENCE

In one of my books on writing speech material I suggest, "Write the end first." A good start promises, a good body of material convinces, but a good ending leaves the impression that you are a professional.

When I showed the "write the end first" chart in class, a young lady asked, "Then if the place catches fire–?" The remark got a laugh, but it is one of the advantages. If you have to close fast, you go into your planned ending, and you finish with honor, even though your coat tails might get singed.

There are other advantages, the ending gives the impression that the group takes home, a good ending explains exactly what you want listeners to do, you avoid the cliche endings, such as, finally–in conclusion–. Any speaker can use those, remember, you're planning to do better.

DEVICES SUCCESSFUL SPEAKERS USE

The descriptions and tips that follow cover a number of the most successful endings. Note how easy each is to use, either for humor or eloquence.

1. *The Assignment:* Let's say the speech is to persuade listeners to assist in the fund drive. A plea, "We need your assistance," is not enough. Tell them specifically what you want them to do. You want them to make three calls on prospective donors. You give them the names and addresses. They start. They know how to ring doorbells, but what do they do next? And what do they say? They greet the prospect, give their name, and explain they are from the church or UA. Now what do they say next? Give them a line that emphasizes the need for funds. Make the job seem as simple as possible. If there is a printed piece on the drive, what do they do with it? Do they show it or hand it to the prospect? What do they say if they show it? How do they answer questions? Since most drives for funds or memberships are serious activities, the assignment close, keep the procedure serious. For a bit of humor admit that the solicitor might meet some prospects who want to argue. When the prospect starts to argue about the need, the solicitor is to say, "The chairman told me not to argue with anybody. I'll just pick up my literature and go." I heard a chairman use this bit, with the promise, "Say this and watch how fast Mr. Hard Nose signs up."

2. *The Summation:* The summation has been mentioned many times in other pages. Sum up the benefits, first why they save time, second why they save labor, and third, why they save money. It is perhaps the easiest way to prove to listeners that you know what you want. I heard a drive chairman say, "We need 79 new members. We have the names of 400 good prospects. One hundred solicitors are working on this. If each worker makes four calls this week, we will have covered all of the prospects, and we will have the 79 new members. All that is asked is four calls from each of you. Make your four calls this week and all we will need then is your attendance at a victory celebration. The date for that is a week from Tuesday."

3. *The Challenge:* The speaker for the hospital drive said, "Back in 1846 six prominent citizens of this town when the population was not quite four hundred souls, decided their town needed a hospital. And you know what they did about it? They went out to the citizens and raised over six thousand dollars for that hospital. Think of that—over 15 dollars for every person living here at the time. That was the start of this hospital. Today the population of our town is over fifty thousand. The facility we plan to build will cost one hundred thousand dollars. That's about two dollars for every person in this town. Where those pioneers got fifteen dollars we are asking you to get two dollars. Can you do it?" This is one type of challenge ending. A challenge lays the problem in the laps of the listeners. You ask if they have the moxie, the guts, the dedication, the commitment. You ask if they have the same fortitude as those pioneers of 1846. Few listeners will admit that those oldsters were better. The challenge can of course be humorous, by proposing the ridiculous, something listeners wouldn't think of doing, or don't want to do. On the serious side, you ask one listener to make a speech on an unfamiliar subject. For instance, you mention Diogenes carrying a candle looking for an honest man. You ask the listener to take this idea, prepare for two minutes and make a two minute speech on what the idea means. You'll find that most listeners in this situation will give the challenge a hard try, and further, most will do quite well. If challenged, they want to do well and they do.

4. *The Review:* The late Al Smith used, "Let's look at the record—" to introduce recitals of what the enemy had not done. I heard a speaker use it thus, "The other party promised you this, and what did you get? They also promised that, and where is it? Further they promised these and did you get them? You did not, all you got was those empty campaign promises. Now these same promisers ask you to return them to office. A vote for them is a vote for progress, they say. Yeah, a vote for them is a vote for oblivion. Why not give them what they gave you—*Nothing.* Vote for our party, we can't do as bad as they did. Show you want action, not alibis." The review fits well at the end of a speech, when the objective is approval or action. It can picture what listeners get for what you ask them to do. These

people who never had access to medical care now have a place they can take their sick to have them examined. When speaking about the failure of others you have a great opening for humor. The same broken promises can arouse emotion. Use it to arouse anger at those responsible, or frustration, and of course determination to throw them out on their ears.

5. *The Question of Series of Questions:* The speaker used the question in his review of the inefficiency of the politicians. The question is good because it asks the listener to pause and think about the answer. In advising the use of questions I have used the six questioning words–*what, why, when, how, where* and *who.* The words give you ideas for six questions such as–

What do you want me to do?
How will I do it?
Why should I do it?

With that list you can fashion scores of questions that will clarify your part in the plan. Note how these question words fit in. Answer the question, "What's this all about?" and you remind the listener.

Answer, "Why should I be interested?" and you again tell him why you are speaking on this subject, and answer his question, "How can I help?" and you have buttoned up.

The question is good to get pledges from workers. Ask, "How many members will you see?" The answer puts the worker on the spot. Ask, "How many dollars will you pledge?" and you'll have a rough estimate of how much money this group will raise. Ask, "When will you make the first call?" and you can stress the immediacy of the need. You may not need all of Kipling's serving men, but you can make your ending more effective by using those that fit in.

6. *The Choice:* Listeners prefer a choice. They don't like to be told there is only one way, and that way is yours. They ask, "What's the alternative?" You might ask the listener to choose between the status quo and your new plan. There are always some who want change. There are others who resent any change. You know how you resent the change the manufacturer made in the package of your favorite cereal. You liked the old

arrangement, why did the dopes change it? If you are proposing a change from today's procedure, organize to explain the benefits of the new and stress them. This will help convince the opponents of change, and it will further sell the ones willing to go along. Give listeners a choice, it is what the salesman does when he asks, "Which do you prefer, the red or the blue?" I heard a speaker use this one, "I am asking you to give ten bucks. You may think you need ten bucks more than the unfortunates it will benefit. If you give it you can bemoan the fact that your ten bucks went down the drain. You can justify a refusal by saying, "There are too many of these requests," or "The money will probably be wasted." But if you give, think of the boost you have given your feelings, you did your bit, you have shown your love of fellow man by your help, you are the kind of person you admire. Some may call you a sucker, but not you. With you, you are tops." Improve the chance of getting action fast by offering a choice.

7. *The Plan of Action:* The speaker says, "We make our first call Sunday afternoon at 3 p.m.!" That is a simple plan of action. If the talk has explained why that time, and given the procedure, those words would need only a plea, "How many of you will be there?" Any plan of action should be simplified. A three step procedure is easy to follow. First, this, second, this, third, this. The ending of the speech is built around the action you want the speaker to follow. I've seen it used by having the listeners recite the first words to say to the prospective donor. They recited only one line, one sentence, but the plan has everybody rehearsing the line. The speaker is in control, he has everybody active, concentrating on the proper approach. The plan of action is used when the drive speaker has two characters demonstrate the solicitation, one acting as the solicitor, the other as the prospect. There is usually some humor in such a demonstration because of the stage fright of the participants, mistakes that may be made, or their asides. The solicitor says, "Hope I don't get many tough prospects like that," or the prospects admit, "I was overpowered." The observer gets some of the enthusiasm needed, saying, "That is easy to do," or "I could do better than that."

8. *The Big Splash, the Climax, the Offer to End All Offers:* This is an ending used in sales meetings. The big splash is saved for last. The sales pitch on the boardwalk is a demonstration of this technique. The speaker describes his food preparation machine and what it will do. The conventioneer says, "My wife would love that." He is hesitating, remembering the reception of the last article he bought for her and brought home from a convention. Then the speaker shows a fountain pen flashlight. The visitor has always wanted a flashlight like that. The flashlight is free if he buys now. Now the speaker shows a small doll that would appeal to anyone. The listener's daughter would love that. It too is free if the conventioneer moves fast. Now comes analysis of the offer, all this for $39.99. The visitor looks in his wallet to see if he has two twenties. The speaker asks, "Who'll be the first?"

The automobile man on TV uses this plan when he sums up the bonuses, the sales manager uses it when he reveals the new product, new offer, or new credit terms. The solicitor uses it when he lists the benefits to the underprivileged or the benefits to the donor. This type of ending allows a speaker to end in high and it can be adapted to most speech subjects. The fund raiser uses the idea when, at the last minute, he reveals that some donor had already given 20% of the amount set as the goal of the drive. The pastor of the church uses it when he reveals that a friend of his in a distant city will give a large amount if the parishioners raise as much as his gift. The promise of bigger and better elephants arouses enthusiasm and brings in the fear of loss. The fund drive workers may need a lift, and the big splash ending can be used to start them thinking of bigger gifts and higher totals.

9. *The Verse or Poem:* One sales expert ended every speech with a poem called the "Little Red Hen." Perhaps you have heard it. It's moral was that the way to success was to stop bellyaching and to keep on scratching. In a talk on listening I heard this ending–

> I've come to the conclusion,
> After giving it a test,
> That the one who listens to me,
> Is the one I like the best.

This four-line bit may be short for a speech ending. Eight lines would perhaps do better. To sum up you might add the moral, "If you like the people who listen to you, why shouldn't others like you because you listen to them?" With that finish the speaker has changed the tempo with the poem and has repeated the point. You'll find many lofty ideas in poetry that most people know. "Breathes there a man with soul so dead?" Think of the adaptations you can make of that line of Sir Walter Scott's for your town, your state, your country, your business, your charity. Then how about the end lines of "Casey at the Bat?" "But there is no joy in Mudville, Mighty Casey had Struck Out." "We can't afford to strike out on this UA drive. Our names would be Mud, our community Mudville if we did." Go on, take it from there. Your verse can be one that brings tears, or humor as you wish. The use of famous lines of poetry lifts the tone of your speech. The use of the laugh poems that you find in the newspapers and magazines fits you into the group. Let the poem express the idea for you. Then button up in your own words, but be short with the button up. Don't let it introduce another speech. Use the idea of the poem as was done in the "Struck out" finish.

10. *The Quotation:* The quotation is easy to come by. There are collections that index quotations so that you can find quotes on almost any subject. The Bible is a great helper. When Cecil B. De Mille was asked why he made so many pictures based on the Bible, he asked, "Why let two thousand years of publicity go to waste?" There is no need for you to let such wealth pass, it is there for you to use, and its familiarity adds force. Not long ago I heard a speaker use the "time" quote from Ecclesiastes, which seemed ideal for his ending. The quote goes, "There is a time to every purpose under the Heaven, a time to be born, a time to die–a time to eat, a time to laugh, a time to mourn, a time to dance–a time to keep silence and a time to speak up." He wanted his listeners to speak up against a proposal of the city council. His tie in went something like this, "This is our time to speak up. Now. Today." You can see why any speaker could use a part or all of that quote to end his speech. You say, "Now is the time." You want action, and you use the quote to give authority to what you say. Think of St. Paul's, "When I was a

child I thought as a child." Read through a few pages in one of the books of quotations and discover how much research compilers have done for you. The famous name quotes that have been used all through the book—such as those of F.D.R., J.F.K., Churchill, the Ancients, Shakespeare, all add authority—came from these books. You might try my system. When I need a quote I look for it in one of the quotation books. One day I needed a quote on "laughter." I found more than 200 entries. Usually the book has three or four possibles. If I do not find one possible to use, I feel the reading has sparked my thinking and I come up with an idea of my own.

11. *The Anecdote:* Often speakers ask me, "Ed, I need a story to end my speech, got one for me?" One that has been popular for years is this classic, "The Hillican asks his boss, "How do you spell rat?"

The boss says, "R–A–T."

"That's not the kind of rat I mean," the other says.

"What kind of rat do you mean?" the boss asks.

"I mean rat like rat now."

Now all the speaker needs is a line, "That's when I am ending this speech, rat now." The applause will start before he moves to sit down.

This story has the point that the speaker for the fund drive wants to make. Workers are to start rat now. The unfortunates dying of hunger want food rat now, they want you to help rat now. Such an idea is catching. If the speaker asks for an answer to his question, "When do you start?" the listeners answer, "Rat now." If the first response is not loud enough, the question can be repeated again and again until the speaker has the whole audience shouting, "Rat now." This illustrates how your story can emphasize the point you want to make. You may want the story to produce only a laugh and allow you to stop talking. Ok, go for the laugh and stop. If you want the story to help make a point as it gets the laugh, follow this plan—

First, state the point
Second, tell the story that illustrates the point
Third, restate the point.

A review of chapter 15 will give you many ideas on the use of stories to make your point and get a laugh or intensify an emotion.

12. *The Stunt:* Having listeners answer "rat now" in answer to the question would be a stunt for most speakers. It is the kind of ending that listeners remember.

Any such stunt needs planning. You need to know what you want the group to do, what you are going to say to get them to do it. Any stunt ending makes your speech different. Handled skillfully it makes you look better. And don't forget Jimmy Durante's line, "They all want to get into the act." Listeners all do. Ask for volunteers and you'll get a line up.

13. *The Quiz:* You've heard speakers talk on dull subjects and you didn't think of them as good speakers. After a dull speech they started to answer questions and became a different person, live, alert, positive, an excellent speaker. If your plan is to close with a question and answer session, help yourself by supplying some questions to the listeners. This will help keep the questions on your objective–humor or emotion. Write your questions on small file cards and have the chairman pass them out. Put a line on the card, "Please do not read the question, just ask the question. Thanks." Another tip is, "Repeat all questions." This gives the questioner a chance to approve your interpretation.

14. *Your Own Standard Ending:* I worked with one factory executive who ended every talk with, "Let me be the first to wish you a Merry Christmas." In the hot days of July or August, the line got him a laugh. "And it gives me terminal facilities with a laugh," he stated. His talks were mainly to retailers and salesmen, visitors who went through his plant. The tour guides gave the group information about the manufacturing. His talks were a friendly gesture to button up the trip to thank the visitors for coming. Fred Palmer, the sales expert, ended all of his speeches with the following:

"Take time to work, it is the price of success,
Take time to think, it is the source of power,
Take time to play, it is the secret of youth,

Take time to read, it is the foundation of knowledge,
Take time to worship, it is the highway of reverence.
Take time to love, it is the sacrament of life.
May the road come up to meet you,
May the wind be always at your back,
and may the good Lord take a likin' to you."

The last three lines, much like the famous Irish blessing, would make a good ending.

The blessing–

"May the road come up to meet you
May the wind be always at your back
May the sun shine warm upon your face
The rain fall soft upon your fields
And until we meet again
May God hold you in the hollow of his hand."

And don't forget the familiar line–

"May the good Lord bless and keep you 'til we meet again."

15. *The Standing Ovation:* I have mentioned this before and have given the advice, "If you want a standing ovation at the end, use an audience participation stunt that has the listeners standing on their feet, doing something." It helps to get their hands above their heads, reaching for the sky, wiggling their fingers, perhaps. Give them fifty seconds to get warmed up, then sit down fast, leaving them on their feet, clapping their hands, shouting and maybe whistling. Then you have your answer when anyone asks, "How did you do?"

YOUR PARTING IMPRESSION

The end of your speech gives listeners the last impression of you. With a minimum of work you can get away from the usual–

"Thank you for listening–"
"That's all I got to say on the subject–"
or Porky Pig's classic–
"That's all folks."

With any of these endings listed you end in high, you leave a good impression, and you slant most ot them at either humor or eloquence.

26

ALL IMPROVEMENT IS SELF-IMPROVEMENT

These chapters have been a blueprint for adding humor and eloquence to your speaking skills. Try out the ideas that you feel comfortable with and see if they work for you. If they work, use them again. If they aren't successful, reject them. That's how speakers improve. They try something, if it works they use it again. If it doesn't work, they forget it. You have been using this "cut and try" system all your life.

BELIEVE THE INSPIRATIONAL SPEAKERS

Cynics may scoff at the statement, "You can do anything you want to do." But that statement has been proven again and again. I say—

you can be humorous
you can be eloquent.

All you need is a strong enough desire to train yourself to be one or both. If you are not humorous or eloquent now, you know you need training. You hear a humorous talk and you might assume that the humorist was born with that knack. You hear an emotional plea and you think that the one who swayed you is especially blessed with the talent to influence groups. Ask either how they developed their skill and their answers will reveal there was no accident of birth or Heavenly gift involved. The formula was "desire plus work." If you are willing to do the work necessary, you can improve. Others have, why not you?

ADVANCEMENT AND RESPECT IS THE PAYOFF

You hear a poor speech and you decide that the speaker's job competence can be measured by his ability to make a good speech. This may not be true, for the speaker's ability to speak may have nothing to do with his job duties. But you can't help feeling that way. You heard the speech and judged what you heard. This is why the ability to speak helps in business. The good speaker is rated higher and so gets chances that the poor speaker does not get. In club and civic work the good speaker can persuade others to work for a cause., join up, donate a fair share or to pick up a banner and carry it in the parade. Speaking ability helps women and men achieve leadership in the groups that help the good causes in our community life.

ADD THE POLISH

You may be an effective speaker today without using humor or eloquence. But if these factors add polish to the speeches you hear, why shouldn't you try for them? These pages have explained how. Try any idea suggested. If it works, keep on trying it until you feel you are expert at it. If it fails, forget it. But don't be discouraged by one or even ten failures. Try other ideas, you'll find many that are naturals for you and you will be a better speaker because of them. Good luck to you and may God bless you.